**this book is from
the kitchen library of**

_____

ALSO BY ART GINSBURG, MR. FOOD®

The Mr. Food® Cookbook (1990)
Mr. Food® Cooks Like Mama (1992)
Mr. Food® Cooks Chicken (1993)
Mr. Food® Cooks Pasta (1993)

MR. FOOD®
makes
dessert

Art Ginsburg
MR. FOOD®

WILLIAM MORROW AND COMPANY, INC.
new york

Library of Congress Cataloging-in-Publication Data

Ginsburg, Art.
Mr. Food® makes dessert / Art Ginsburg.
p.   cm.
Includes index.
ISBN 0-688-11602-7
1. Desserts.   2. Baking.   I. Title.   II. Title: Mr. Food®
makes dessert.
TX773.G49 1993
641.8'6—dc20   93-8492
CIP

Printed in the United States of America

First Edition

1   2   3   4   5   6   7   8   9   10

BOOK DESIGN BY CHARLOTTE STAUB

Dedicated to
All those in food and on stage
Who've worked as hard as I have—
And have yet to realize their dreams,
as I have

acknowledgments

Anybody who thinks a cookbook is simply a collection of recipes thrown together should think again!

It's work, by a lot of people. Well, for instance . . .

My wife, Ethel, who not only helps with the recipe testing, but keeps me in line, too.

My son, Steve, who heads up everything for my books and handles everything that I could possibly think of—and everything else, too! He's the real boss.

My daughter-in-law, Carol, and daughter Caryl Gershman, who organize and make sense of the recipes and all of my words. Each time my scattered thoughts come together to become an entertaining, easy-to-follow book . . . it's because of Carol and Caryl.

Linda Rose, Steve Gershman, Alan Roer, Madeline Burgan, and Loriann Bishop, my recipe testers who test and test until we're all certain that the recipes will work every time. Boy, do they have patience!

And Mary Ann Oliver! She types, copies, sorts, and does hundreds of things for us all, so that everything comes out right.

Roy Fantel and Tammy Ginsburg, who check up on all of us with their fine-tooth combs.

Chuck Ginsburg, Flo Toppal, Dan Wolk, and Bill Treacy, who make sure that we all have what we need at our fingertips, right when we need it.

I must also thank my agent, Bill Adler, without whose creativity, foresight, and guidance I wouldn't have written my books; and my editor, Maria Guarnaschelli, who, with a smile on her face and in her voice, encourages and supports me as she leads me to book-writing happiness; and Al Marchioni, Phyllis Heller, Skip Dye, and Larry Norton, the gang at William Morrow who push harder for me than I do for myself—they're not only a publishing group, they're dedicated friends.

And there are more! But these people never get their names on the books like I do; they never get the credit they deserve . . . Well, gosh! They just did, and am I glad—'cause to all these guys I owe a really big THANKS!

Thanks, also, to the companies, friends, and viewers who've graciously shared their recipes with me, including:

Keebler®
Chilean Fresh Fruit Association
Entenmann's
Hellmann's & Best Foods Mayonnaise
Borden, Inc.
The North Carolina Department of Agriculture
Quaker Corn Meal
The Florida Department of Agriculture
Kellogg USA
Bisquick®, a registered trademark of General Mills, Inc.
North American Blueberry Council
Texas Fresh Promotional Board
Pepperidge Farm, Inc.
Kraft/General Foods, Inc.
Chocolate Riesen® Caramels
Valley Grower Magazine
McCormick®/Schilling®
California Prune Board
Steve Gershman
Barbara McMullen
Michael Cocca
Linda Rose
Alan Roer
Joan Talbert
Portia Farkas
Hannah Rosenthal
Miriam Grode

Minnie Katz
Jackie Stundel
Sharon J. Karpovich

Recipes courtesy of *Homemade Good News Magazine* and Savannah Foods & Industries, Inc., makers of Dixie Crystals Sugar: Chocolate on Chocolate Pie, Sugar Cookies, Brown Sugar Brownies, and Peach Frosty.

contents

introduction

Ah, desserts! Everybody's treats! Time to get excited by the chocolates, the creams, the fruits, cakes, pies, cookies, and the rest of the goodies.

Desserts are the crowning toppers of any meal, but let's not forget to enjoy them as snacks and rewards—or anytime you want "ooh"s and "aah"s and squeals and swoons!

One of the questions I'm most often asked is, "What can I make for a quick dessert? I'm having company and I need something special." This book answers that—because we want to give our guests a treat—a feeling that we're doing something special for them. But it's not only guests whom we want to please—it's us and our families, too.

Sure, these days we're being more careful about what we eat, but we still want and deserve the special pleasure of satisfying our sweet tooth.

Many of these quick and easy recipes are from my TV show; viewers often write to thank me for them.

And many of these are ones that I've thanked viewers for sending to *me*—because they've worked out so well. They're shortcuts, favorites, and even family secrets.

Now, you won't find recipes here that take lots of steps, hundreds of ingredients, or proofing, or waiting. You won't find desserts that'll make so much of a mess in your kitchen that cleaning up becomes a big chore. Uh uh!

All of these can be made from ingredients found on your supermarket shelves or in your own cupboards. . . . No-nonsense, everyday, easy-to-come-by favorites.

And you'll certainly find an assortment of flavor choices—and flavor combinations. There are chocolate desserts, peanut butter desserts, and everything in between, including combinations using each—and both. WOW!!

And there are recipes for apples, berries, peaches, plums, bananas, and whatever's in season, handy and sensible. And when fresh isn't available, or it's too expensive, you can almost always use frozen or canned, whichever fits, to still make the dessert come out right. Who could possibly object to having all these options?!

You know I always want to have lots of options, and with all of today's convenience foods, we've got them! We have instant puddings and gelatins, whipped toppings, cakes from mixes, ready-made frostings, glazes, and pie shells. Now we can make so many things that years ago took hours of preparation and baking time—and cleanup time, too.

With our busy life-styles, and so many two-income and single-parent families, most of us don't have the time, money, or inclination to spend all day in the kitchen—and we don't have to. Sure, things started from scratch are often fuller-tasting and better quality, but with all the convenience items available, we can still make treats that have our own unique touches.

Better products, with better quality and better taste, are being developed every day. Whenever a new item is introduced, there are purists who continue to insist on making their own "from scratch." There's nothing wrong with that, but after a while, most of them realize that these items make sense. And why not?

Keep in mind that even most food professionals use shortcuts or convenience foods in one form or another. From using nonstick cookware to doughnut, bread, and other mixes, there are lots of things out there that really help us all. Convenience is the way to go!

Now, about health . . .

Generally, the recipes are "as they came out best." If a recipe calls for salt, sugar, butter, or anything that you can't have, make your own sensible substitutions. Because so many people are watching their diets today, where I could I've indicated some easy substitutions, like yogurt for sour cream. I've even included some yummy low-fat recipes that call for prune purée instead of oil. You won't believe how "normal-tasting" and good they are!

I hope that you can treat yourself a bit every once in a while, but in any case, you should definitely CHECK WITH YOUR DOCTOR FIRST.

I also hope that you'll always remember to do your own thing with my recipes. Whether you follow the instructions exactly or make your own creations of prepared desserts by simply drizzling with chocolate syrup, topping with sprinkles, whipped topping, or ice cream, you can make the simplest dessert tempting and fancy, without spending a bunch of money. And don't forget, there's never any problem with serving our abundant, better-than-ever-tasting fresh fruit as a dessert, either. With all the sweet varieties available all year long, it's always a dessert champion.

So, again, here are over one hundred popular, quick, and easy sweets, as they are. Have fun with them, so that you'll hear "ooh"s and "aah"s and squeals and swoons and be applauded for causing them!

And, finally, I guarantee that this book will not get a chance to collect dust on your bookshelf. It's gonna be at your elbow, on your counter, ready to help answer your needs. So, if you use it just for ideas, that's fine. Any way you do it, you'll still be a kitchen hero! That should make you very happy. And when you're happy, I'm happy, 'cause you know what happy people say. . . . Yup,

OOH it's so GOOD!!™

charts
and
information

baking "bits"

Often an oven does not have even heat distribution; the sides or bottom of the oven may be hotter than the center or upper shelf. To ensure even baking and crust color, baking items should be rotated or shifted from one place to another within the center of the oven.

If the cake sticks to the pan during removal, do not force it out. Instead, return the pan to the oven to heat it slightly; then remove it from the oven and run the edge of a knife around the sides of the pan to free the cake. Lift the pan and tap it gently against a table to release any part of the cake that may be sticking to the bottom of the pan. Then turn the pan over and tap the bottom again with a knife to release the cake from the pan. To avoid this problem, be sure to grease the pan evenly and completely, then dust it with flour. An even better method is to place a circle of parchment or baking paper, measured to the size of the pan, on the pan bottom after it has been greased. This replaces the need to dust with flour.

general baking suggestions

- Use clean, dry (or greased and floured, as necessary) pans.
- Do not overcrowd ovens.
- Do not move cakes while they are still soft.
- Do not slam the oven door during baking.
- Always use oven mitts when moving hot pans.
- Cupcakes will take less time to bake than a cake of the same batter.
- Finished cakes will shrink slightly from the sides of their pans and will spring back when pressed lightly with a finger.
- Allow cakes to cool on a rack for 5 to 10 minutes before turning out.

(Cake left in pans too long will become soggy.) Allow cakes to stand an additional 5 to 10 minutes before frosting.
• Do not store cakes in boxes until completely cooled.

storage

• If freezing baked goods, place the date and name of the item on the wrap.
• It is best to freeze cakes uniced. Some icings, especially the ones made with sugar, corn syrup, water, etc., will sweat, and moisture will condense on the surface.
• Baked goods may be iced while still frozen.
• If storing in the refrigerator, cover tops of baked goods with a layer of waxed paper.
• To prevent drying out, wrap the cake with suitable wrapping material like aluminum foil, plastic wrap, or waxed paper.

the "deal" on desserts

When a **cake** bakes, a chemical reaction occurs, transforming the unbaked ingredients into a new solid entity. The word "cake" is from Middle English, and from the earliest days of civilization, people have considered it a food for the gods as well as for themselves.

In America, **pies** are most often desserts; what we call dessert pies the English call tarts, since they eat many more meat pies than we do. Early traditions involved eating mince pies to ensure prosperity, and, in the early twentieth century, it was even claimed that you could judge a nation's strength and prosperity by its pies! Those most associated with the United States are pumpkin, molasses-flavored shoofly, and apple pie.

Cookie is an American word, derived from the Dutch word meaning "small cake." The English call our cookies "biscuits." Because there are so many options for ingredients, flavorings, textures, shapes, and sizes, there are more varieties of cookies than any other baked product.

common baking terms

Beat	To make a mixture smooth and introduce air by a brisk regular motion that lifts the mixture over and over. Usually done with an electric mixer.
Blend	To mix two or more ingredients so that each loses its individual identity. Usually done with an electric mixer.
Combine/Mix	To join together two or more ingredients. Usually done by hand.
Cream	To work foods, alone or with other ingredients, until soft and fluffy. Usually applied to shortening and sugar. Done by stirring, rubbing, or beating with a spoon or electric mixer.
Cut	To incorporate butter, margarine, or solid shortening into dry ingredients with the least amount of blending, with the mixture ending up in small particles. Done by hand.
Fold in	To mix food gently, without releasing air bubbles. Usually done by hand, by scooping to the bottom center of the bowl via the side of the bowl and bringing bottom ingredients up over the top ingredients, until the foods are lightly combined. This method is done when it's necessary to keep individual ingredients intact, such as when adding nuts or chocolate morsels to a batter or when adding chocolate to whipped cream. It's also used to achieve a marbled effect.
Stir	To use continuous movement to either combine ingredients, or to keep something from burning. Usually done by hand.
Whip	To beat into a froth, as with eggs or cream. Usually done with an electric mixer.

ingredient substitutions

EQUALS

1 tablespoon cornstarch	2 tablespoons flour *or* 1⅓ tablespoons minute tapioca
1 cup corn syrup	1 cup granulated sugar plus ¼ cup water
1 cup honey	1¼ cups granulated sugar plus ¼ cup water
1 ounce chocolate	1 square or ¼ cup cocoa plus ½ tablespoon shortening
1 cup butter	1 cup margarine
1 cup milk	½ cup evaporated milk plus ½ cup water *or* ⅓ cup nonfat dry milk plus water to make 1 cup
1 teaspoon baking powder	¼ teaspoon baking soda plus ½ teaspoon cream of tartar *or* ¼ teaspoon baking soda plus ½ cup fully soured milk *or* ¼ teaspoon baking soda plus ¼ to ½ cup molasses
1 cup sour cream	3 tablespoons melted butter stirred into buttermilk or yogurt to make 1 cup
1 cup heavy cream	⅓ cup melted butter plus ¾ cup milk
Ricotta cheese	Cottage cheese, liquid drained

weights and measures

	EQUALS
Dash	less than ⅛ teaspoon
3 teaspoons	1 tablespoon
4 tablespoons	¼ cup
5 tablespoons plus 1 teaspoon	⅓ cup
8 tablespoons	½ cup
10 tablespoons plus 2 teaspoons	⅔ cup
12 tablespoons	¾ cup
16 tablespoons	1 cup
2 tablespoons	1 fluid ounce
1 cup	½ pint or 8 fluid ounces
2 cups	1 pint or 16 fluid ounces
4 cups	2 pints or 1 quart or 32 fluid ounces
4 quarts	1 gallon or 64 fluid ounces
Juice of 1 lemon	about 3 tablespoons
Juice of 1 orange	about ½ cup
Grated peel of 1 lemon	about 1½ teaspoons
Grated peel of 1 orange	about 1 tablespoon

1 POUND* OF	EQUALS APPROXIMATELY
Flour	4 cups
Cornmeal	3 cups
Sugar	2 cups
Brown sugar	3 cups
Confectioners' sugar	2½ cups
Raisins	3 cups

*One pound equals 16 ounces avoirdupois (our usual standard of weight measurement).

packaged foods note

As with many processed foods, package sizes may vary by brand. Generally, the sizes indicated in these recipes are average sizes. If you can't find the exact indicated package size, whatever package is closest in size will usually do the trick.

cakes

easy fudge pudding cake

4 to 6 servings

Homemade chocolate cake and pudding, without any fuss.
Sound too good to be true? Well,
here it is, and is it ever fudgy!

1 cup biscuit baking mix	¼ cup plus ½ cup chocolate-flavored syrup
¼ cup baking cocoa	
1 can (14 ounces) sweetened condensed milk, divided	1 teaspoon vanilla extract
	½ cup hot water

Preheat the oven to 375°F. In a large bowl, mix together the biscuit baking mix and cocoa, then stir in 1 cup sweetened condensed milk, ¼ cup chocolate syrup, and the vanilla extract; blend well. Spoon the mixture evenly into a greased 8-inch square baking pan. In a small bowl, combine the remaining sweetened condensed milk, ½ cup chocolate syrup, and water. Pour the liquid mixture over the cake mixture. *Do not stir.* Bake for 30 to 35 minutes or until the center is set and the cake begins to pull away from the sides of the pan. Remove from the oven and let stand for 15 minutes. Spoon into dessert dishes, spooning pudding from the bottom of the pan over the top.

NOTE: Serve warm with whipped cream, whipped topping, or ice cream. Refrigerate leftovers if there are any! (Told ya it was easy!!)

java chocolate cake

about 12 servings
(with 2 cups Coffee Cream)

*Looking for the perfect dessert for a party or
special dinner? Here it is!*

1 box (18.25 ounces) devil's food cake mix
4 eggs
1 cup sour cream
¼ cup vegetable oil
1 package (4-serving size) instant chocolate pudding and pie filling
¼ cup water
¼ cup coffee liqueur
1 package (6 ounces) semisweet chocolate chips

COFFEE CREAM

2 cups frozen whipped topping, thawed (an 8-ounce container equals 3½ cups)
1 teaspoon instant coffee
2 tablespoons coffee liqueur

Preheat the oven to 350°F. Place the cake mix, eggs, sour cream, oil, pudding mix, water, and coffee liqueur in a large bowl. Mix on medium-high speed or by hand until thoroughly blended. Fold in the chocolate chips. Turn into a well-greased 12-cup Bundt pan and bake for 45 to 50 minutes. Cool for 20 minutes, then remove from pan. Meanwhile, in another bowl, fold together the ingredients for the Coffee Cream. When ready to serve, spoon a dollop over each slice of cake.

low-fat chocolate fudge cake

about 9 servings

So smooth, they'll say it's sinful . . . but it's not,
because it really is low in fat.
That's right. Great taste without egg yolks or butter.

1	cup water	1	cup plus 2 tablespoons sugar
½	cup prune purée or prepared prune butter	¾	cup baking cocoa
3	large egg whites	1½	teaspoons baking powder
1½	teaspoons vanilla extract	¼	teaspoon baking soda
1	cup plus 2 tablespoons all-purpose flour	¼	teaspoon salt

Preheat the oven to 350°F. In a large bowl, combine the water, prune purée, egg whites, and vanilla extract. Beat to blend thoroughly. Add the remaining ingredients and mix completely. Spread the batter into an 8-inch square baking dish that has been coated with nonstick vegetable spray. Bake for about 30 minutes or until a wooden toothpick inserted in the center comes out clean. Cool on rack. Cut into squares.

NOTE: Prune purée and prune butter are available ready to use (found in the jam and jelly or baking section of your supermarket), or you can make your own purée by combining 1⅓ cups (8 ounces) pitted prunes and 6 tablespoons water in the container of a food processor; pulse on and off until the mixture is smooth. It makes 1 cup.

lemon pudding cake
about 12 servings

*This is moist and yummy as is—or you can easily make it
another fruit flavor, or even chocolate! It's a great recipe
for experimenting with, so go ahead
and be creative—it'll work.*

1 package (18.25 ounces) yellow cake mix	4 eggs
1 package (4-serving size) instant lemon pudding and pie filling	⅔ cup vegetable oil
	⅔ cup water

Preheat the oven to 325°F. In a large bowl, blend together all ingredients on a low speed until moistened, then beat at medium speed for 2 minutes. Pour into a 12-cup Bundt pan that has been generously coated with nonstick vegetable spray. Bake for 50 to 60 minutes or until a toothpick inserted in the center comes out clean. Turn out onto a serving plate while still warm but not hot.

NOTE: You can get nice color and flavor variations by using any color/flavor gelatin dessert mix, or even instant chocolate pudding mix, instead of the lemon pudding. And if you'd like to top it with a simple glaze, just mix together ¾ cup confectioners' sugar, 1 tablespoon lemon juice, and 2 teaspoons water. Drizzle that over the top and sides of the cake.

caramel pear cake

about 16 servings

It's so much easier today to get the tastes of old-fashioned homemade. I mean—spice cake, fresh pears, caramel topping . . . Mmmm!! Old-fashioned enough??

1 package (18.25 ounces) spice cake mix

2 fresh pears, pared, halved, cored, and thinly sliced

GLAZE

½ cup firmly packed brown sugar

2 tablespoons all-purpose flour

2 tablespoons water

¼ cup chopped almonds

¼ cup melted butter

Prepare the cake mix according to the package directions and bake in a 9" × 13" baking pan. Arrange the sliced pears on top of the hot cake. In a medium-sized bowl, mix together the glaze ingredients. Spoon the glaze over the pears. Place the cake under the broiler, about 3" from the heat, broiling until the pears are thoroughly heated and the top is bubbly.

NOTE: If the glaze hardens before it is spooned over the cake, rewarm it in the microwave or on the stove, until smooth. If you'd like to vary the taste a bit, use pecans for a Louisiana praline touch or pistachios for a special California touch.

bananas foster crunch cake

about 12 servings

*Want to make your family feel pampered? Well, it's a snap
to do with this easy-as-can-be special dessert.*

CAKE

½ cup (1 stick) margarine, softened

1½ cups granulated sugar

2 eggs

1¼ cups mashed ripe banana (about 4 medium-sized bananas)

¼ cup light or dark rum

1 teaspoon vanilla extract

1½ cups all-purpose flour

¾ cup cornmeal

1½ teaspoons baking powder

½ teaspoon baking soda

½ teaspoon salt

STREUSEL TOPPING

⅓ cup all-purpose flour

⅓ cup chopped pecans

¼ cup firmly packed brown sugar

1½ tablespoons margarine, softened

Preheat the oven to 350°F. In a large bowl, beat together the margarine and sugar until crumbly-fluffy. Add the eggs, one at a time, beating well after each addition. Mix in the banana, rum, and vanilla extract. In a separate bowl, combine the flour, cornmeal, baking powder, baking soda, and salt; blend well. Add the flour mixture to the margarine mixture and stir just until blended. Pour the mixture into a well-greased 12-cup Bundt pan. In a small bowl, combine all the Streusel Topping ingredients. Sprinkle the top of the cake batter with Streusel Topping. Bake for 45 to 55 minutes or until a wooden toothpick inserted in the center comes out clean. Cool for 10 to 15 minutes, loosen sides, invert on a serving tray, and remove pan.

peach pound cake

about 16 servings

Who can turn down pound cake? And with peaches?!
There's enough to make the whole gang cheer,
'cause you make this one in a Bundt pan.

1 cup (2 sticks) margarine or butter, softened

3 cups sugar

6 eggs at room temperature

1 teaspoon vanilla extract

3 cups all-purpose flour

¼ teaspoon baking soda

½ teaspoon salt

½ cup sour cream

2 cups peeled and chopped peaches (4 to 6 peaches)

Preheat the oven to 350°F. In a large bowl, cream together the margarine and sugar until light and fluffy. Add the eggs, beating well. Stir in the vanilla extract. In another large bowl, combine the flour, baking soda, and salt. Stir the flour mixture into the egg mixture. Add the sour cream and beat on low until the mixture is smooth. Gently fold in the peaches. Pour the batter into a well-greased and floured 12-cup Bundt pan. Bake for 70 to 80 minutes or until a wooden toothpick inserted in the center comes out clean. Turn onto serving plate while still warm (but not hot!).

NOTE: This also works great with nectarines or apples.

melon chiffon cake

about 12 servings

So light and different, it's a good thing this makes a family-sized cake. They've never heard of melon cake? Even after they taste it they won't believe it! It's that good.

1 medium-sized cantaloupe	Melon balls for garnish (optional)
¼ cup water	
1 box (14½ ounces) angel food cake mix*	Sprigs of mint for garnish (optional)

Preheat the oven to 350°F. Seed, slice, and peel the melon. Cut into chunks and place in blender or food processor. Purée enough to make 1½ cups, discarding any remaining purée. Combine the purée and the water. Empty the contents of the egg-white packet from the cake mix into a large bowl. Blend in the purée mixture. Beat on highest speed for about 20 minutes, until stiff peaks form and a trench cut through the egg whites with a spatula will hold its shape. Reduce speed to low and sprinkle in the cake flour mixture just until thoroughly mixed. Pour into a greased 12-cup Bundt pan and bake for 25 to 30 minutes or until the crust is golden brown, and is firm to the touch. Invert the pan on a wire rack to cool. When cooled completely, run a knife around the edges, pull cake away from sides of pan, remove from pan and place on serving plate. Refrigerate until ready to serve.

NOTE: This cake is great served plain, but if you want to use a topping, try confectioners' sugar, whipped cream or whipped topping, a Berry Sauce (see page 106), or a drizzle of Chocolate Sauce (see page 105).

*Quick-mix and instant-rise angel food cake mixes do not produce good results. Use only those mixes requiring at least 5 to 10 minutes whipping time for egg-white mixture.

no-shortening pineapple cake

about 30 pieces

*These days, most people want less fat in their diets. Here's
a dessert that has less fat, but not less taste. Really!
(I didn't believe it either, until I tried it myself!)*

2 cups all-purpose flour

2 cups sugar

2 eggs, beaten

2 teaspoons baking soda

1 teaspoon vanilla extract

1 cup chopped nuts

1 can (20 ounces) crushed
pineapple, undrained

Preheat the oven to 350°F. In a large bowl, mix together the
flour and sugar. Add the remaining ingredients and mix well. Pour
the mixture into an ungreased 9" × 13" baking dish. Bake for 45
to 50 minutes or until a wooden toothpick inserted in the center
comes out clean. Cool completely before topping.

NOTE: Serve topped with fresh, canned, or frozen fruit, a sprinkle
of confectioners' sugar, or Cream Cheese Frosting (see page 110).

paradise fruit cake

about 15 servings

Indulge yourself in this treat of tropical flavors!
It'll sure remind you of those
soft beach breezes.

1 box (18.25 ounces) yellow
cake mix

2 boxes (4-serving size) instant
vanilla pudding and pie
filling

1 can (20 ounces) crushed
pineapple in juice

1 cup sugar

4 small bananas, sliced

1 container (8 ounces) frozen
whipped topping, thawed

Prepare the cake mix according to the package directions, and bake in a 9" × 13" baking pan. Allow to cool slightly. Meanwhile, make the pudding according to the package directions and set aside. In a small saucepan over medium heat, cook the pineapple with the sugar for 5 minutes, or until the sugar is dissolved. Pour the pineapple mixture over the warm cake; let cool. Place banana slices over the pineapple; cover with the pudding, then the whipped topping.

NOTE: Top with nuts, cherries, and coconut, if desired.

amazin' raisin cake

about 12 servings

Remember when Grandma used to spend all day in the
kitchen? The smells were heavenly! Now enjoy
that same homemade comfort
but with "today easy."

3	cups all-purpose flour	2	eggs
2	cups sugar	1	cup mayonnaise
2	teaspoons baking soda	3	cups peeled, cored, and chopped apples (4 to 5 apples)
1½	teaspoons ground cinnamon		
1	teaspoon pumpkin pie spice	1	cup raisins
½	teaspoon salt	1	cup coarsely chopped walnuts
⅓	cup milk		

Preheat the oven to 350°F. In a large bowl, mix together the flour, sugar, baking soda, cinnamon, pumpkin pie spice, and salt. Add the milk, eggs, and mayonnaise. Beat with an electric mixer at low speed for about 2 minutes or until well blended, scraping the bowl frequently. The batter will be thick. Add the apples, raisins, and walnuts and mix completely with a wooden spoon. Spoon the mixture into a greased and floured 9" × 13" baking dish. Bake for 40 to 50 minutes or until a wooden toothpick inserted in the center comes out clean. Remove the cake from the oven and cool in the pan for about 10 minutes. Then remove the cake from the pan and cool completely on a wire rack.

NOTE: Serve this with whipped topping or your favorite frosting. And by the way, light mayonnaise will work as well as regular.

apple snack cake

16 to 24 servings

We all love to snack on fresh apples. If you're looking for another way to enjoy them, try this easy "snack" cake.

¾ cup vegetable oil

2 eggs

2 cups sugar

2½ cups all-purpose flour

1 teaspoon baking soda

1 teaspoon baking powder

1 teaspoon salt

1 teaspoon ground cinnamon

3 cups peeled, cored, and coarsely chopped apples (4 to 5 medium-sized apples)

1 cup coarsely chopped pecans

Preheat the oven to 350°F. In a large bowl, combine the oil, eggs, and sugar; beat with an electric mixer at medium speed until mixed well. In another large bowl, combine the flour, baking soda, baking powder, salt, and cinnamon. Add the flour mixture to the oil mixture, stirring until well blended. Fold in the apples and pecans. Spread the batter into a 9" × 13" greased baking dish. Bake for about 60 minutes or until a wooden toothpick inserted in the center comes out clean. Cool slightly, then cut into serving-size pieces.

apple upside-down cake

about 12 to 15 servings

Another delicious way to use those apples that'll have everybody coming back for more. (No, you don't have to stand on your head to make it!)

3 medium-sized tart apples, peeled, cored, and cut into ¼-inch slices

1 cup apple cider or juice plus extra for cake mix

⅓ cup (5⅓ tablespoons) butter or margarine

1 cup firmly packed brown sugar

10 to 12 maraschino cherries, cut in half

½ cup chopped walnuts

1 package (18.25 ounces) spice cake mix

Preheat the oven to 350°F. In a medium-sized saucepan, simmer the sliced apples in 1 cup cider for about 5 minutes, or just until tender. Drain, reserving the apple cider. Combine 2 tablespoons reserved, warm cider with butter and brown sugar in a 9" × 13" baking pan that has been coated with nonstick vegetable spray. Bake for 5 minutes; remove from the oven and stir the mixture. Arrange the apple slices and cherry halves in the brown sugar mixture. Sprinkle with walnuts; set aside. Prepare the cake mix, substituting apple cider for the water that is called for in the package directions. Pour the batter into the pan over the sugar-nut mixture. Bake for 55 to 60 minutes. Remove from the oven and invert on a serving platter; let stand for about 1 minute, then remove the pan. (Rearrange apple slices and cherries, if necessary.) Serve warm.

NOTE: This is great as is or served with some whipped topping.

raisin pumpkin cake
about 12 servings

*This is really rich, yet amazingly low in fat. So go ahead
and indulge. It's full of good stuff.*

2   cups all-purpose flour

2   teaspoons baking powder

1   teaspoon baking soda

½   teaspoon salt

2   teaspoons pumpkin pie
     spice

2   cups granulated sugar

4   eggs

1   can (1 pound) or 2 cups
     pumpkin

¾   cup prune purée or prepared
     prune butter

2   cups all-bran cereal

1   cup raisins

1   cup chopped nuts

Preheat the oven to 350°F. In a large bowl, mix the flour, baking powder, baking soda, salt, pumpkin pie spice, and sugar. Set aside. In another large bowl, beat the eggs until foamy. Add the pumpkin, prune purée, and cereal; mix well. Add the flour mixture, mixing only until combined. Stir in the raisins and nuts. Spread the mixture evenly in a 10" × 4" tube pan that has been coated with nonstick vegetable spray. Bake for about 1 hour and 5 minutes, or until a wooden toothpick inserted near the center comes out clean. Cool completely before removing from the pan.

NOTE: If you'd like, you can finish this off by dusting it with confectioners' sugar. Prune purée and prune butter are available ready to use (found in the jam and jelly or baking section of your supermarket), or you can make your own purée by combining 1⅓ cups (8 ounces) pitted prunes and 6 tablespoons water in the container of a food processor; pulse on and off until mixture is smooth. It makes 1 cup.

pumpkin layer cake

about 12 servings

Once you've tried this, you'll agree that pumpkin isn't just for Halloween. It's so special, you can't pass it up!

CAKE

3 eggs

1 cup granulated sugar

2/3 cup canned pumpkin

1 teaspoon lemon juice

1/2 cup all-purpose flour

1 teaspoon baking powder

2 teaspoons ground cinnamon

1 teaspoon ground ginger

1/2 teaspoon ground nutmeg

1/2 teaspoon salt

1/2 cup chopped walnuts plus extra for garnish

1/4 cup confectioners' sugar

FILLING

1 cup confectioners' sugar

1 package (8 ounces) cream cheese, softened

4 tablespoons (1/2 stick) butter, softened

1/2 teaspoon vanilla extract

Preheat the oven to 375°F. In a large bowl, combine all Cake ingredients and mix with an electric mixer until smooth. Pour onto a well-greased and lightly floured 9" × 13" cookie sheet. Sprinkle the walnuts over the batter. Bake for 12 to 15 minutes or until a wooden toothpick inserted in the center comes out clean.

Meanwhile, sprinkle a dish towel with 1/4 cup confectioners' sugar. Run a knife around the edge of the cookie sheet to loosen the baked cake, invert the cake onto the towel, and let it cool slightly. Remove the pan, then allow the cake to cool completely. Meanwhile, place all Filling ingredients in a medium-sized bowl; beat until smooth. Cut the cake crosswise into thirds, turning the pieces nut side up. Spread filling onto each of the 3 pieces of cake, dividing it evenly. Sprinkle a little granulated sugar on a serving tray (to keep the cake from sticking). Place one layer on the prepared tray, then stack the remaining layers over it. Sprinkle extra walnuts on top. Chill, then cut into slices.

christmas crunch cake

12 to 16 servings

*Your holiday gathering will be extra special, with very little
extra work. And when there's no baking? Wow!!
(Your refrigerator does the work overnight!)*

1   package (8 ounces) cream
    cheese, softened

1¼ cups confectioners' sugar

1   container (15 ounces)
    ricotta cheese

1   cup miniature semisweet
    chocolate chips

1   container (8 ounces) or
    1 cup finely chopped red
    candied cherries

1   Louisiana or other ring
    crunch cake (20 to 24
    ounces)

1   container (8 ounces) frozen
    whipped topping, thawed

¾ cup halved red candied
    cherries, for garnish

In a large bowl, beat together the cream cheese and confectioners' sugar until fluffy, about 2 minutes. Stir in the ricotta cheese
until well blended, then fold in the chocolate chips and chopped
cherries. Chill the mixture overnight, so it achieves the proper firm
spreading consistency. The next day, carefully cut the cake horizontally, making three layers. Set the bottom layer on a serving
plate. Spread ⅓ of the chilled mixture on top of the bottom layer,
then add the next cake layer and repeat until the top of the cake
is covered but the sides are not. Spread whipped topping on the
sides of the cake so that it meets the filling on top of the cake.
Garnish by placing cherry halves around the cake edge.

scotch spice cake

15 to 18 servings

This sounds a little more exotic, a little bit different—
you won't believe how easy it is
until you read on.

1 package (4-serving size)
  instant butterscotch pudding
  and pie filling

2 cups milk

1 package (18.25 ounces)
  spice cake mix

½ cup chopped peanuts

Preheat the oven to 350°F. In a large bowl, combine all the ingredients except the peanuts; mix well. Add the peanuts; mix again. Place in a greased and floured 9" × 13" baking pan. Bake for 30 to 35 minutes or until a wooden toothpick inserted in the center comes out clean.

holiday cake
8 to 10 servings

*This is a quick, festive way to top your holiday meal.
(And they'll think you fussed for hours.)*

1 prepared angel food cake (about 10 ounces)

8 egg whites at room temperature

1 tablespoon vanilla extract

½ cup sugar

1 candy cane

Preheat the oven to 350°F. Place the cake on a baking sheet. In a large bowl, beat the egg whites and vanilla extract with an electric mixer on medium speed until soft peaks form. Gradually add sugar at high speed and beat until stiff peaks form. Frost the cake with the egg-white mixture (meringue) and bake for 10 to 12 minutes. Place the candy cane in a plastic bag and seal. Break into small pieces with a hammer. When the cake is cooled, place it on a cake plate and sprinkle with the crushed candy cane.

NOTE: This cake will remain fresh for 3 to 4 days.

pies and tarts

candy apple pie

6 to 8 servings

*Remember candy apples from when you were a kid? You
know—you got them at carnivals and at the circus.
If you'd like to bring back that same special
taste without all the sticky mess, here's
a pie that'll do it for you.
(Everybody will wink
at the taste, too.)*

1¾ cups unsweetened apple juice, divided

⅓ cup cinnamon candies (about 15 candy disks)

¼ teaspoon red food color

½ teaspoon vanilla extract

4 tart cooking apples, peeled, cored, and thinly sliced

3 tablespoons cornstarch

1 prepared 9-inch graham cracker pie crust

1½ cups frozen whipped topping, thawed (1 8-ounce container equals 3½ cups)

½ teaspoon ground cinnamon

In a large saucepan, combine 1½ cups apple juice, candies, food color, vanilla extract, and apples. Bring to a boil, then simmer just until the apples are tender, about 10 to 15 minutes, stirring frequently. Combine the remaining ¼ cup juice and cornstarch. Stir into the apple mixture and continue to cook until thickened, about 2 minutes, then cook for another 2 to 3 minutes. Remove from heat; cool to room temperature. Spread the apple filling over the bottom of the pie crust. Chill for several hours or until the filling holds its shape. Before serving, combine the whipped topping and cinnamon; top each slice with a dollop of the mixture.

NOTE: Granny Smith and Rome apple varieties work best here.

plum pie

6 to 8 servings

"Plum Pie?" you ask? Sure! It's a nice change.
Very fresh tasting . . .

2   cans (16 ounces each)
    whole plums in syrup,
    drained and pitted (2 cups)

¼ cup water

½ cup sugar

¼ cup cornstarch

¼ teaspoon salt

1   unbaked 9-inch pie shell

CRUMB TOPPING

⅓ cup all-purpose flour

⅓ cup sugar

½ teaspoon ground cinnamon

¼ teaspoon ground nutmeg

3   tablespoons butter or
    margarine

Preheat the oven to 350°F. Place the plums and water in a large saucepan; boil, covered, for 4 to 5 minutes. Add ½ cup sugar, cornstarch, and salt and cook for about 5 minutes more or until thick and clear, stirring occasionally. Cool the mixture, then pour into the unbaked pie shell. In a medium-sized bowl, mix together the Crumb Topping ingredients; sprinkle evenly over the pie. Bake for 35 to 40 minutes or until the crumbs are golden and the plum filling is bubbly.

NOTE: This Crumb Topping goes great with any fruit pie.

"blue-bana" cream pie

10 to 12 servings

For years I've been asked how to make a simple blueberry pie where the berries stay nice and crunchy. Here's a creamy version that's easy, crunchy, and a whole lot more.

1 package (8 ounces) cream cheese, softened

1 cup sugar

2 envelopes (from a 2.6-ounce box) whipped topping mix

2 bananas, sliced

1 prepared 10-inch graham cracker pie crust (extra-serving size)

Lemon juice

1 can (21 ounces) blueberry pie filling

1 cup fresh blueberries

In a large bowl, combine the softened cream cheese and sugar with an electric beater until well blended. Prepare the whipped topping, 1 envelope at a time, according to the specific package directions, and fold into the cream cheese mixture. Place slices of banana evenly over the crust, sprinkle with some lemon juice (to keep the bananas from turning black), and spoon the cream mixture over the bananas. In a medium-sized bowl, combine the blueberry pie filling and fresh blueberries. Top the pie with the blueberry mixture. Refrigerate for at least 4 hours before serving.

one-dish strawberry pie

6 to 8 servings

Want to use more of the luscious, inexpensive, in-season strawberries that are in the market? Here's a delicious and simple way to enjoy them.

1   quart strawberries, rinsed
½   cup biscuit baking mix
¾   cup sugar
2   tablespoons butter or margarine, softened
2   eggs

1   can (12 ounces) evaporated milk
⅛   teaspoon red food color
2   teaspoons vanilla extract
Whipped cream or whipped topping for garnish

Preheat the oven to 350°F. Reserve 1 cup whole strawberries for garnish; slice the remaining berries. In a blender, purée 1¾ cups berries to yield 1 cup puréed berries. Add the biscuit baking mix, sugar, butter, eggs, and evaporated milk to the blender. Stir slightly to mix the ingredients together. Blend on high for 1 minute. Stir in the remaining sliced berries, food color, and vanilla extract. Pour into a greased 9-inch deep-dish pie plate. Bake for about 55 minutes or until a knife inserted in the center comes out clean. Cool; garnish with whipped cream and the remaining whole berries.

NOTE: Yes, it forms its own crust!

strawberry cream pie

6 to 8 servings

*Here's a homemade treat that takes only minutes to prepare.
Why, they'll spend more time raving about it than
you took putting it together!*

1 package (4-serving size)
vanilla instant pudding and
pie filling

1 cup sour cream

¼ cup milk

2 teaspoons grated orange or
lemon rind

2 cups frozen whipped topping,
thawed (plus extra for
garnish, if desired) (1 8-
ounce container equals 3½
cups)

1 prepared 9-inch graham
cracker pie crust

1 pint fresh strawberries,
hulled, rinsed, and patted
dry, plus extra for garnish

In a large bowl, combine the vanilla pudding mix, sour cream, milk, and orange rind. Add the whipped topping and beat with a wire whisk for 1 minute or until well blended. Spoon half the mixture into the pie crust. Press the strawberries, stem-side down, into the mixture, then top with the remaining mixture. Freeze the pie for about 1 hour or refrigerate for 3 hours before serving. Garnish with additional whipped topping or strawberries.

pumpkin crunch cream pie

6 to 8 servings

Don't have time to bake, but want something a little special?
This should solve your problem!

¾ cup cold milk

1 package (4-serving size) instant vanilla pudding and pie filling

½ cup canned solid-pack pumpkin

¾ teaspoon pumpkin pie spice

⅔ cup slivered almonds

⅔ cup semisweet chocolate chips

1 container (8 ounces) frozen whipped topping, thawed, divided

1 prepared 9-inch graham cracker pie crust

Pour the milk into a large bowl, add the pudding mix, and beat with a wire whisk until well blended, about 1 minute. Let stand for 5 minutes. Blend in the pumpkin, pumpkin pie spice, almonds, chocolate chips, and 2 cups of the whipped topping. Spoon the mixture into the pie crust; chill for at least 4 hours. Before serving, garnish with additional whipped topping.

NOTE: You can use your own homemade crust, if you prefer. And if you'd really like to add a special touch, also garnish the pie with chocolate curls, which you can make by shaving a bar of chocolate with a knife.

yogurt pumpkin pie

12 to 16 servings

*We usually think of pumpkin pie only in autumn and during
the winter holidays, but with this light twist on the
classic seasonal dessert, they're going to want
it in every season.*

2 prepared 9-inch graham
cracker pie crusts

1 teaspoon water

1 egg white

2 eggs, lightly beaten

1 container (8 ounces) plain
yogurt

1 can (16 ounces) solid-pack
pumpkin

1 teaspoon vanilla extract

1 cup evaporated milk

¾ cup sugar

¼ teaspoon ground cloves

¼ teaspoon ground ginger

1 teaspoon ground cinnamon

¼ teaspoon ground nutmeg

Preheat the oven to 375°F. Place the pie crusts on cookie
sheets. In a small bowl, beat together the water and egg white.
Brush onto the pie crusts and bake for about 5 minutes or until
the crusts are light golden. Cool thoroughly. Meanwhile, place the
lightly beaten eggs in a large bowl; add the remaining ingredients
and stir until thoroughly mixed. Pour into the cooled pie crusts,
place the pies on the cookie sheets, and bake for 50 to 60 minutes
or until a wooden toothpick inserted in the center comes out clean.
Cool completely. Store in the refrigerator.

NOTE: Serve with whipped cream or whipped topping.

chocolate on chocolate pie

6 to 8 servings

Here's how to take an old favorite and make it even
more special by adding just one simple step.
Chocolate on chocolate . . . Mmmm!

1 cup sugar

½ cup (1 stick) unsalted butter
  or margarine, melted

¼ cup cornstarch

2 large eggs

1 teaspoon vanilla extract

1 package (6 ounces)
  semisweet chocolate chips

1 cup chopped pecans

1 unbaked 9-inch chocolate pie
  shell

Preheat the oven to 350°F. In a large bowl, combine the sugar, butter, cornstarch, eggs, and vanilla extract; mix well. Stir in the chocolate chips and pecans. Pour the mixture into the pie shell. Bake for about 40 minutes or until the filling begins to pull away from the sides of the crust. Cool completely on a rack.

NOTE: Serve with a dollop of whipped cream or whipped topping and a drizzle of chocolate syrup, if you'd like. You can use your own homemade pie shell or buy one already prepared—whatever you prefer.

impossible chocolate cream pie

6 to 8 servings

No flour to get all over, no dough to roll, only one bowl to wash, no long time in the kitchen, and still a lot of oohs! and aahs! Impossible?? Not at all—try it!

2 eggs

1 cup milk

¼ cup (½ stick) butter or margarine, softened

2 squares (1 ounce each) unsweetened chocolate, melted and cooled

1 cup sugar

1 teaspoon vanilla extract

½ cup biscuit baking mix

Preheat the oven to 350°F. Combine all the ingredients in a blender and blend on high for 1 minute. Pour the mixture into a greased 9-inch pie plate. Bake for 30 minutes or until set. Cool completely before serving.

NOTE: Serve topped with whipped cream, nuts, cherries, or chocolate sprinkles.

chocolate silk pie

8 servings

*Be prepared—it's so silky and elegant, your guests
won't leave till they've finished every bite!*

1 prepared 9-inch butter-
flavored pie crust

1 teaspoon water

1 egg white

1 package (4-serving size)
instant vanilla pudding and
pie filling

1 package (4-serving size)
instant chocolate pudding
and pie filling

¼ teaspoon ground nutmeg

¼ teaspoon ground cinnamon

1 cup milk

2 cups softened vanilla ice
cream

3 tablespoons whipped
topping, for garnish

1 small chocolate bar,
crushed, for garnish

Preheat the oven to 375°F. Place the pie crust on a cookie
sheet. In a small bowl, beat together the water and egg white. Brush
on the pie crust and bake for about 5 minutes or until the crust is
light golden. Cool thoroughly. Meanwhile, in a large bowl, place
the puddings, nutmeg, cinnamon, milk, and softened ice cream;
mix for about 1 minute with an electric mixer or until the mixture
is smooth. Pour the mixture into the cooled pie crust and freeze
for a few hours until firm. Remove from the freezer about 15
minutes before serving. Garnish with whipped topping and crushed
chocolate. Store leftover pie in the freezer.

simple cheesecake pie

6 to 8 servings

*The name says it all—as simple as can be! And it's great as is
or topped with berries, pineapple, or whipped cream.*

3 packages (8 ounces each)
cream cheese, softened

1 jar (7½ ounces)
marshmallow fluff

3 tablespoons all-purpose flour

½ teaspoon vanilla extract

½ teaspoon lemon juice

2 eggs

1 prepared 9-inch graham
cracker pie crust

Preheat the oven to 350°F. In a large bowl, beat together the
cream cheese, fluff, flour, vanilla extract, and lemon juice until
smooth. Add the eggs, one at a time, just until mixed. Pour into
the pie crust and bake for about 45 minutes or until the edges start
to brown. Turn off the oven and let the cheesecake cool in the
oven with the door cracked open for 1 hour. Refrigerate for at least
4 hours before serving.

no-bake cheesecake

6 to 8 servings

*Enjoy this one any time of the year, 'cause there's no baking!
It'll have them (and you) cheering.*

1 package (8 ounces) cream cheese, softened	2 teaspoons vanilla extract
½ cup sugar	1 container (8 ounces) frozen whipped topping, thawed
1 cup (½ pint) sour cream	1 prepared 9-inch graham cracker pie crust

In a large bowl, beat the cream cheese until smooth; gradually beat in the sugar. Blend in the sour cream and vanilla extract. Fold in the whipped topping until well mixed. Spoon the mixture into the crust. Chill for 4 to 5 hours to set. Keep refrigerated.

NOTE: This is nice garnished with your favorite fresh fruit or pie filling, or sprinkled with crumbled chocolate cookies.

double chocolate no-bake cheesecake

6 to 8 servings

Not a chocolate lover? Taste this and you will *be!*

1 cup semisweet chocolate chips

1 package (8 ounces) cream cheese, softened

¼ cup (½ stick) butter, softened

½ cup sugar

⅓ cup sour cream

¼ teaspoon almond extract

1 cup heavy cream

1 prepared 9-inch chocolate-flavored pie crust

Melt the chocolate chips in a double boiler over simmering water or place in a microwavable bowl and microwave on high (full power) for 1 to 1½ minutes or until melted; set aside to cool. In a large bowl, beat the cream cheese, butter, and sugar until smooth and fluffy. Add the sour cream, almond extract, and cooled melted chocolate; beat until well mixed. In a small chilled bowl, whip the heavy cream until stiff. Fold by hand (not with an electric mixer) into the chocolate mixture. Spoon into the chocolate-flavored pie crust and smooth the top with a spatula. Chill until firm. Keep refrigerated.

NOTE: Serve with sprinkled cocoa, shaved chocolate, or toasted almonds over dollops of additional whipped cream.

black forest cheesecake

6 to 8 servings

Chocolate and cherries . . . what a great combination!
Here's a cheesy twist with those favorite flavors.
It sure is an easy way to be fancy.

1 package (8 ounces) cream
cheese, softened

¾ cup sugar

2 squares (1 ounce each)
semisweet chocolate, melted

1 teaspoon vanilla extract

2 eggs

1 prepared 9-inch butter-
flavored pie crust

1 can (21 ounces) cherry pie
filling

Preheat the oven to 325°F. In a small bowl, beat the cream cheese until fluffy. Add the sugar, chocolate, vanilla extract, and eggs; mix well. Place the crust on a baking sheet. Pour the mixture into the crust. Bake for 35 minutes or until the filling springs back when touched lightly. Cool on a wire rack. Spread the cherry pie filling over the top. Chill until ready to serve.

easy pumpkin cheesecake
10 to 12 servings

*There's something special about "autumn" desserts. We sure
seem to crave them, especially when the temperature
drops and the leaves start to change color. Well,
here's one that doesn't add a lot of work to
your busy fall schedule. (And the best
part is that you can enjoy this
one any time of the year!)*

1 egg yolk plus 2 whole eggs

1 prepared 10-inch graham cracker pie crust (extra-serving size)

2 packages (8 ounces each) cream cheese, softened

¾ cup sugar

1 can (16 ounces) solid-pack pumpkin

1½ teaspoons ground cinnamon

½ teaspoon ground ginger

Preheat the oven to 350°F. Beat the egg yolk and brush on the pie crust. Bake the crust for 5 minutes; set aside. In a large bowl, combine the 2 eggs, cream cheese, and sugar, and beat with an electric beater on medium speed until smooth. Add the pumpkin, cinnamon, and ginger and continue beating until well blended. Spoon the mixture into the prepared pie crust and bake for 40 to 45 minutes or until set. Let cool, then refrigerate for several hours or overnight.

NOTE: This is great plain, but I usually add a dollop of whipped cream or a scoop of ice cream. Mmmm!!

italian cheese pie

6 to 8 servings

*A comforting, "old country" favorite that's sure to
win lots of new fans. Yes, it's like Mama's.*

6 eggs	2 teaspoons grated lemon rind
½ cup sugar	1 unbaked 9-inch deep-dish
½ teaspoon vanilla extract	pie shell
1½ pounds (2½ cups) ricotta cheese	

Preheat the oven to 350°F. In a large bowl, beat the eggs with the sugar, vanilla extract, ricotta cheese, and grated lemon rind until well blended. Pour into the pie shell and bake for about 70 minutes or until the cake is done and the edges are golden. Cool before cutting.

NOTE: Don't worry if the cake falls slightly—it usually does! You can sprinkle the top with confectioners' sugar, if you'd like.

sour cream pie

6 to 8 servings

*Here's a no-fail, anybody-can-whip-it-up pie
that's sure to please.*

1 cup (½ pint) sour cream

1 package (8 ounces) cream
  cheese, softened

⅓ cup sugar

2 teaspoons vanilla extract

1 container (8 ounces) frozen
  whipped topping, thawed

1 prepared 9-inch graham
  cracker pie crust

In a large bowl, combine the sour cream, cream cheese, sugar, and vanilla extract; mix well. Fold in the whipped topping, then pour the mixture into the pie crust. Chill for at least 2 hours before serving.

NOTE: Use your own homemade pie crust or buy one already prepared, whichever you prefer.

krispy cream pie

6 to 8 servings per pie

*Sometimes a little twist on an old "popular" can turn it
into a new "excitement"—like this one!*

CRUST

⅓ cup peanut butter

½ cup white corn syrup

2 heaping cups Rice
Krispies® cereal

FILLING

½ gallon vanilla or coffee ice
cream, softened*

¼ cup peanut butter

In a large bowl, mix together all the crust ingredients and pat into the bottom of two 8-inch pie plates. (Hint: Keep fingers wet, so they won't stick to the crust.) In another large bowl, mix together the filling ingredients; spoon into the crusts, dividing the filling evenly between the 2 pie plates. Place the pies in the freezer to set.

NOTE: Drizzle with chocolate syrup before serving, if desired.

*Be sure to soften the ice cream to a creamy, not liquid, consistency before using it and freeze the final product right away. To soften the ice cream, break it up in a bowl and stir with a wooden spoon. **Do not let the ice cream melt.** To save time, I sometimes use a peanut butter ice cream instead of mixing the ice cream and peanut butter together.

"mom's vacation" dessert

6 servings

*On vacation from the kitchen? You can still have a cool
and refreshing dessert, 'cause anybody
can make this one in a flash.*

3 ounces frozen lemonade
concentrate, thawed (1 small
can equals 6 ounces)

1 cup frozen whipped topping,
thawed (1 8-ounce container
equals 3½ cups)

⅔ cup sweetened condensed
milk (1 can equals 14
ounces)

½ pint fresh strawberries or
blueberries for garnish

1 package (6 tarts) graham
cracker tart shells

In a large bowl, fold together the lemonade, whipped topping, and sweetened condensed milk. Spoon into the tart shells. Top with fresh berries or other fruit. Serve immediately or after chilling, whatever you prefer.

banana sundae tarts

12 servings

It's your turn to have the gang over and you don't know what to make for dessert?? Try this. After all, everybody loves banana sundaes, and you'll love how easy these are.

1 package (4-serving size) instant vanilla or French vanilla pudding and pie filling

2 cups milk

2 medium-sized ripe bananas, sliced

2 packages (6 each) graham cracker tart shells

½ cup semisweet chocolate chips

2 tablespoons half-and-half

Whipped cream for garnish

Chopped nuts for garnish

Maraschino cherries or fresh strawberries for garnish

In a medium-sized bowl, mix together the pudding mix and milk; beat on low speed with an electric beater for 1 to 2 minutes, until smooth. Fold in the bananas and pour the mixture into the tart shells, dividing the mixture evenly between shells. Refrigerate for 20 minutes or until set. Meanwhile, in a small saucepan, combine the chocolate chips and half-and-half and cook over a low heat, stirring until smooth. Spoon the mixture over the prepared tarts. Before serving, garnish with whipped cream, nuts, and cherries.

NOTE: No tart shells on hand?? Use one 9-inch graham cracker pie crust.

blueberry tarts

6 servings

*When blueberries are in season, we're all looking for extra ways
to enjoy them. So when the blueberries are plentiful and the
price is a bargain, pick up an extra pint and try this.*

3 cups fresh blueberries, plus
extra for garnish, if desired

¼ cup orange juice

¾ cup sugar

3 tablespoons cornstarch

1 package (6 shells) graham
cracker tart shells

Whipped cream or whipped
topping for garnish (optional)

In a blender, purée 1½ cups blueberries and the orange juice.
In a small saucepan, combine the puréed blueberry mixture, sugar,
and cornstarch. Cook over a medium heat until thickened; remove
the blueberry sauce from the heat and let cool. Place about ¼ cup
fresh blueberries in each tart shell. Completely cover the fresh berries with thickened, cooled sauce. Serve plain or top the tarts with
a dollop of fresh whipped cream or whipped topping and some
fresh berries.

NOTE: If you want, you can use shortcake shells instead of the
graham cracker shells.

cookies and bars

meringue cookies

about 24 cookies

Light, yet loaded with rich flavor—why, these
are downright heavenly!

2 egg whites (at room
   temperature)
½ teaspoon vanilla extract

⅓ cup sugar
⅓ cup miniature semisweet
   chocolate chips

Preheat the oven to 325°F. In a large bowl, beat the egg whites and vanilla extract with an electric mixer until soft peaks form. Gradually beat in the sugar; beat until stiff peaks form. Fold in the chocolate chips. Drop by tablespoonfuls onto a nonstick cookie sheet that has been coated with nonstick vegetable spray. Bake for 10 minutes. Turn off the oven but leave the cookies in the oven until cool.

soft molasses cookies

about 4 dozen

Here's something a little different. Remember Mama's molasses cookies? Try these . . . they're just as soft and rich-tasting as we remember.

1 cup sugar	½ cup cold water
½ cup vegetable oil	1 teaspoon ground cloves
1 egg	1 teaspoon ground cinnamon
1 teaspoon baking soda	3½ cups all-purpose flour
½ cup molasses	

Preheat the oven to 350°F. In a large bowl, mix together the sugar, shortening, and egg. Dissolve the baking soda in 1 tablespoon hot water and add to the sugar mixture. Add the molasses, cold water, cloves, and cinnamon; mix well. Add the flour gradually, mixing well. Drop by teaspoonfuls onto ungreased cookie sheets and bake until firm, no more than 10 minutes. Remove from the cookie sheets and let cool.

cookies and bars

butter cookies
about 4 dozen

*Everybody loves butter cookies, so what nicer way
to let them know you care?*

1 cup (2 sticks) butter, softened	1 tablespoon vanilla extract
1 cup confectioners' sugar, divided	2¼ cups all-purpose flour
	¼ teaspoon salt
	¾ cup chopped nuts (any kind)

Preheat the oven to 400°F. In a large bowl, cut in all ingredients, except ½ cup confectioners' sugar, until well mixed and a soft ball forms. Roll the mixture into small balls and place on 10" × 15" cookie sheets that have been coated with nonstick vegetable spray. Bake for 10 to 12 minutes or until just light golden. While still warm (not hot), roll in the remaining ½ cup confectioners' sugar.

pudding cookies
about 2 dozen

These are fun to make and fun to eat, so have the kids help make them. (We know they'll help eat them!)

1 cup biscuit baking mix

1 package (4-serving size) instant pudding and pie filling, any flavor

1 egg

¼ cup vegetable oil

Sugar for sprinkling

Preheat the oven to 350°F. In a large bowl, mix together all ingredients. Roll the batter into balls and place on ungreased non-stick cookie sheet(s), 2 inches apart. Flatten the cookies with a fork and sprinkle with sugar. Bake for 12 minutes or until golden.

soft peanut butter cookies

about 2 dozen

*This is my kind of baking—quick, and with great results,
'cause who doesn't like peanut butter?!*

1 cup sugar	1 egg
1 cup creamy peanut butter	1 teaspoon vanilla extract

Preheat oven to 325°F. In a medium-sized bowl, mix all the ingredients together thoroughly. Drop the mixture by teaspoonfuls onto a nonstick baking sheet and press a crisscross pattern into each drop with a fork. Bake for about 10 minutes or until light golden. Cool before removing from the baking sheet.

NOTE: For a little variety, try pressing colored candies like M & M's® into the cookies immediately after removing them from the oven. Kids of all ages love them! And in case you were wondering, I'm absolutely sure that no flour is necessary in this recipe.

sugar cookies

about 3 dozen

*Always a "sweet" way to enjoy some time with the kids
or the grandkids—fun for everybody!*

3 cups all-purpose flour

2 teaspoons baking powder

¼ teaspoon salt

½ cup vegetable shortening

1 cup sugar, plus extra for sprinkling

1½ teaspoons grated lemon rind

2 eggs, well beaten

1 tablespoon heavy cream or milk

Preheat the oven to 425°F. In a medium-sized bowl, combine the flour, baking powder, and salt. In a large bowl, cream together the shortening and sugar until light and fluffy. Add the lemon rind, eggs, and heavy cream; beat thoroughly. Gradually add the flour mixture and blend. Roll the dough into a thin sheet (about ¼-inch thick) on a lightly floured board. Cut rounds with a cookie cutter and sprinkle with extra sugar. Bake on nonstick cookie sheet(s) for 6 to 8 minutes or until light golden. Remove from cookie sheet(s) immediately and place on a rack to cool.

sponge cookies
about 3 dozen

Here's an old-fashioned cookie with a new-fashioned twist—
they're so quick and easy to make (and to eat!).

3 egg whites, well beaten	½ teaspoon vanilla extract
⅓ cup confectioners' sugar	⅓ cup all-purpose flour
2 egg yolks	½ teaspoon baking powder

Preheat the oven to 350°F. Place the egg whites in a large bowl and beat until stiff; gradually add in the sugar. In a small bowl, beat the egg yolks until lemon colored, then add to the egg-white mixture and continue beating. Add the vanilla extract; beat again. In another bowl, combine the flour with the baking powder, then fold into the egg mixture. Cover cookie sheet(s) with waxed paper. Spoon the mixture onto the waxed paper, forming 3-inch-long finger-shaped cookies, and bake for 8 to 10 minutes or until light golden. Cool slightly, then remove from the pan with a spatula.

NOTE: Sprinkle with confectioners' sugar or serve with fresh strawberries and whipped topping and you've got an easy, old-fashioned dessert.

brown sugar brownies
12 to 16 servings

Want an old-time taste of heaven? Here it is! (Better make extra . . . 'cause you can't stop eating these!)

½ cup (1 stick) butter, softened to room temperature

2 cups dark brown sugar

2 eggs, well beaten

1 cup all-purpose flour

1 teaspoon baking powder

1 teaspoon vanilla extract

1 cup pecan pieces

Confectioners' sugar for sprinkling (optional)

Preheat the oven to 325°F. In a large bowl, cream the softened butter; add the sugar and eggs. Mix thoroughly; add the flour and baking powder and blend. Add the vanilla and nuts. Pour the mixture into a well-greased 8-inch square baking pan and bake for 35 to 40 minutes. Cool in the pan, then cut into squares and sprinkle with confectioners' sugar.

NOTE: If these bake a little longer, don't worry. They're good that way, too, but not as chewy.

graham cracker treats

about 2 dozen squares

*These really are "treats." They're so chocolaty,
they practically melt in your mouth.*

1 box (13½ ounces) graham cracker crumbs (4 cups)	1 package (6 ounces) chocolate chips
1½ teaspoons vanilla extract	1 can (14 ounces) sweetened condensed milk
	Pinch of salt

Preheat the oven to 350°F. In a large bowl, mix together all the ingredients. Heavily grease a 9" × 13" glass baking dish and press the mixture in evenly. Bake for 20 to 25 minutes or until the top just starts to brown. Cut into squares and immediately remove from the baking dish. The squares will harden as they cool.

apple nut bars
21 bars

Have a few apples left over? Are they starting to get soft?
Here's a way to use them that's sure to be popular.

1 cup all-purpose flour	¼ cup melted margarine
1 cup granulated sugar	⅓ cup raisins
½ teaspoon salt	1 cup chopped nuts
¼ teaspoon baking powder	1 cup finely chopped apples
2 eggs, well beaten	

Preheat the oven to 350°F. In a large bowl, mix together the flour, sugar, salt, and baking powder. Add the remaining ingredients and mix well. Place the batter in a greased 9" × 13" baking pan. Bake for 40 to 50 minutes or until the edges are golden. Remove from the oven and cut into bars while still warm, not hot.

NOTE: Before serving, you might want to roll the bars in confectioners' sugar or spread with a cream cheese frosting. Maybe serve them with whipped topping as a "dip" or serve plain as a great snack cookie.

apple scrounge

8 to 10 servings

*Silly name, I know—but that's part of the fun. Everybody'll
want to know what it is and how to make it. But
most of all, they'll want to eat it.*

6 cups peeled and cored apple
slices (about 6 to 7
medium-sized apples)

1 cup chopped walnuts

¾ cup honey

1 cup apple cider or juice

TOPPING

½ cup (1 stick) butter or
margarine

1½ cups all-purpose flour

¼ teaspoon salt

1 teaspoon ground cinnamon

3 tablespoons brown sugar

Preheat the oven to 400°F. Place the apple slices in a greased
9" × 13" baking pan. Sprinkle with nuts, drizzle with honey, and
pour cider on top. In a medium-sized bowl, make the Topping by
cutting the butter into the flour (working together with a fork) until
coarse like cornmeal; mix in the salt, cinnamon, and brown sugar.
Sprinkle the Topping over the apples. Bake, covered, for 30
minutes or until the apples are soft. Uncover and bake for 10
minutes more or until the edges turn light golden brown. Serve
warm.

NOTE: For an extra-special treat, put a little ice cream or sour cream
on top before serving.

lemon squares

24 to 30 squares

For light, lemony flavor that lingers . . . these are the best.
(One of my most-requested recipes!)

CRUST

2   cups all-purpose flour

½ cup confectioners' sugar

½ pound (2 sticks) butter, softened

1   teaspoon lemon rind

FILLING

4   eggs, well beaten

2   cups granulated sugar

3   tablespoons all-purpose flour

½ teaspoon baking powder

¼ cup lemon juice

1   tablespoon lemon rind

1   tablespoon confectioners' sugar for topping

Preheat the oven to 350°F. In a large bowl, mix together the 2 cups flour with the ½ cup confectioners' sugar. Cut in the butter, working it in well with a fork, stir in the 1 teaspoon lemon rind, then pat the mixture into a greased 9" × 13" baking pan to make a crust. Bake for about 20 minutes or until golden. Meanwhile, in another large bowl, combine all the Filling ingredients. Mix well, then pour onto the hot crust. Bake for another 20 minutes. Remove from the oven. Pour the remaining 1 tablespoon confectioners' sugar through a hand strainer over the baking pan, distributing it evenly over the top. Cut into squares while still warm. Refrigerate, then serve.

cookies and bars

halloween bars

24 to 36 bars

You won't be able to resist when your little ghosts and goblins request these time after time. Why, they can make any day a holiday!

½ cup (1 stick) butter or margarine

1½ cups graham cracker crumbs

1 can (14 ounces) sweetened condensed milk

1 package (12 ounces) semisweet chocolate chips

1 cup peanut butter chips

Preheat the oven to 350°F. Place the butter in a 9" × 13" baking dish and melt in the oven. Remove the dish from the oven and distribute the melted butter evenly over the bottom. Sprinkle the graham cracker crumbs evenly over the melted butter; pour the sweetened condensed milk evenly over the crumbs. Top with the chocolate chips and peanut butter chips; press down firmly. Bake for 25 to 30 minutes or until lightly browned. Cool, then cut into bars.

oatmeal bars

about 21 bars

Want to bring a smile to everybody's face? Here's an old-fashioned goody that Mom used to whip up fast . . . and it's still fast!

1½ sticks (¾ cup) butter or margarine

1 tablespoon maple or maple-flavored syrup

1 teaspoon baking soda

½ teaspoon ground allspice

2 cups rolled oats (uncooked oatmeal)

1 cup all-purpose flour

1 cup sugar

¼ cup chocolate chips or raisins (optional)

Preheat the oven to 350°F. Melt the butter and syrup over a low heat on the stovetop or in the microwave. In a large bowl, combine the butter mixture, baking soda, and allspice; mix well and let cool. Add the rolled oats, flour, sugar, and chocolate chips, if desired; mix well. Press the dough into a 9" × 13" glass baking dish that has been coated with nonstick vegetable spray. Bake for 15 minutes. Cut into bars immediately; recut after the bars cool completely.

cookies and bars

breads and muffins

banana bread

1 loaf

*I've tried lots of banana breads, and this
one is my newest favorite.*

½ cup vegetable oil

1 cup sugar

2 eggs, lightly beaten

3 ripe bananas, mashed

2 cups all-purpose flour

1 teaspoon baking soda

½ teaspoon baking powder

½ teaspoon salt

3 tablespoons milk

½ teaspoon vanilla extract

Preheat the oven to 350°F. Place the oil in a large bowl. Gradually add the sugar while beating lightly. Add the eggs and continue beating. Add the mashed bananas and beat just until moistened. Set aside. In a separate bowl, combine the flour, baking soda, baking powder, and salt. Add the dry mixture to the banana mixture and beat just until moistened. Add the milk and vanilla extract and continue beating just until mixed. Pour the mixture into a greased and floured 9" × 5" loaf pan and bake for 50 to 60 minutes or until a wooden toothpick inserted in the center comes out clean. Let cool in the pan on a wire rack for about 10 minutes. Turn out onto the rack and cool completely.

blueberry lemon loaf

1 loaf

What a great combination of flavors!

2	cups all-purpose flour	1½	cups sugar
1½	teaspoons baking powder	2	eggs
¼	teaspoon salt	⅓	cup milk
¼	teaspoon ground nutmeg	2	teaspoons lemon rind
½	cup (1 stick) margarine or butter, softened	2	cups fresh or frozen blueberries, thawed and drained

Preheat the oven to 350°F. In a large bowl, mix together the flour, baking powder, salt, and nutmeg; set aside. Place the margarine and sugar in another large bowl; beat at medium speed until light and fluffy. Add the eggs and beat well. Add the flour mixture and milk and beat at low speed until the mixture is smooth. Stir in the lemon rind and blueberries. Pour the mixture into a lightly greased 9" × 5" loaf pan and bake for 60 to 70 minutes, or until a wooden toothpick inserted in the center comes out clean. Let cool in the pan for 10 minutes.

strawberry bread
1 loaf

Nothing says "Home" better than a fresh-baked bread. Say it easily and better with fresh or frozen strawberries.

1 cup frozen unsweetened whole or fresh strawberries

Sugar for sprinkling plus 1 cup sugar

1½ cups all-purpose flour

1½ teaspoons ground cinnamon

½ teaspoon salt

½ teaspoon baking soda

⅔ cup vegetable oil

2 eggs

⅔ cup chopped walnuts

Place the strawberries in a medium-sized bowl; sprinkle lightly with the sugar. Slice the berries. (If frozen, let the berries stand until thawed, then slice.) Preheat the oven to 350°F. Grease and flour a 9" × 5" loaf pan. In a large bowl, combine the 1 cup sugar, flour, cinnamon, salt, and baking soda; mix well. Blend the oil and eggs into the strawberries; add to the flour mixture. Stir in the walnuts, blending until the dry ingredients are just moistened. Pour the batter into a prepared pan and bake for 50 to 60 minutes, or until a wooden toothpick inserted in the center comes out clean. Let cool in the pan on a rack for 10 minutes. Turn the loaf out of the pan and cool completely.

cherry nut bread

2 loaves

*This cake-type bread is perfect for adding novelty to
your table, or just for snacking.*

2½ cups all-purpose flour

1¼ to 1½ cups sugar (to taste)

1 tablespoon baking powder

7 tablespoons vegetable
shortening

3 eggs

1 cup orange juice

2 tablespoons grated
orange peel

¼ cup cherry juice (from the
canned cherries)

1 can (1 pound) tart cherries,
well drained and coarsely
chopped

½ cup chopped nuts

Preheat the oven to 350°F. In a large bowl, combine the flour,
sugar, and baking powder. Cut in the shortening. Stir in the eggs,
orange juice, orange peel, and cherry juice. Fold in the cherries
and nuts. Pour into 2 greased and floured 8" × 4" loaf pans. Bake
for 45 minutes or until a wooden toothpick inserted in the center
comes out clean. Cool for 10 minutes, then remove from the pan.
Cool on a rack or serve warm.

NOTE: Why not enjoy one loaf now and freeze the other? It freezes
well.

applesauce bread

1 loaf

Serve plain for a snack, or top with whipped cream or ice cream for a fancy dessert. Both are great ways to enjoy this nice, moist bread.

2 cups whole wheat flour	1½ cups applesauce
1 teaspoon baking soda	⅔ cup sugar
½ teaspoon baking powder	¼ cup vegetable oil
1 teaspoon ground cinnamon	2 eggs
½ teaspoon ground nutmeg	¼ cup milk

Preheat the oven to 350°F. Sift together the flour, baking soda, baking powder, cinnamon, and nutmeg. In a large bowl, combine the applesauce, sugar, oil, eggs, and milk; mix well. Add the dry ingredients and beat well. Pour into a greased 9" × 5" loaf pan. Bake for 1 hour or until a wooden toothpick inserted in the center comes out clean. Remove from the pan; cool on a wire rack.

NOTE: I like it a little sweeter, so I add an additional ⅓ cup sugar. You can also use skim milk instead of regular.

easy banana muffins

about 15 muffins

One little homemade touch can make a whole meal special.
Just whip these up—they'll really perk up
your bread basket or dessert tray.

½ cup (1 stick) butter, softened

1 cup sugar

2 eggs, beaten

3 ripe bananas, mashed

1¼ cups all-purpose flour

½ teaspoon baking soda

Preheat the oven to 350°F. In a large bowl, combine the butter and sugar and beat well. Add the eggs and beat the mixture until light and fluffy. Stir in the bananas. In a medium-sized bowl, combine the flour and baking soda; add to the banana mixture, stirring just enough to moisten the dry ingredients. Lightly grease and flour muffin pans, then fill ⅔ full with batter. Bake for 25 minutes or until a wooden toothpick inserted in the center comes out clean. Great served warm.

spicy carrot muffins

24 medium-sized muffins

*Muffins are "in." They make a great snack all by themselves
or a tasty addition to any meal. Either way, you'll
feel great giving your family some
homemade goodness.*

2 cups all-purpose flour	1 cup flaked coconut
1¼ cups firmly packed brown sugar	½ cup chopped pecans or walnuts
1 tablespoon pumpkin pie spice	3 eggs, beaten
2 teaspoons baking soda	1 cup vegetable oil
½ teaspoon salt	½ teaspoon vanilla extract
2 cups shredded carrots	Granulated sugar for topping

Preheat the oven to 375°F. In a large bowl, combine the flour, brown sugar, pumpkin pie spice, baking soda, and salt. In a separate large bowl, combine the remaining ingredients, except granulated sugar; mix well. Add the carrot mixture to the flour mixture, stirring until moistened. Line 24 muffin cups with paper baking cups; spoon the mixture into the cups. Sprinkle the tops with granulated sugar. Bake for 18 to 20 minutes or until a wooden toothpick inserted in the center comes out clean. Remove from the pans and cool on wire racks.

NOTE: Serve with butter, margarine, or cream cheese—whatever!

puddings, sauces, and other yummies

esteban's flan

8 servings

Just like what you'd enjoy in sunny Mexico . . .
and OOH it's so BUENO!!

3 tablespoons plus ¼ cup
sugar, divided

6 eggs, beaten

1 teaspoon vanilla extract

2 cups half-and-half

Pinch of salt

Preheat the oven to 350°F. Place the 3 tablespoons sugar in a 9-inch glass pie plate and place in the oven for 15 to 20 minutes or until liquid and golden, stirring occasionally so it doesn't burn. Meanwhile, place the remaining ingredients in a large bowl and beat well. Pour the egg mixture over the melted sugar and place the pie plate in a large pan. Place hot tap water in the larger pan to halfway up the sides of the pie plate. Bake for 40 to 45 minutes or until a wooden toothpick inserted in the center comes out clean. Cool, then slice into wedges and serve with the sauce from the pie plate spooned over it.

chocolate bread pudding
8 to 9 servings

*Never heard of this one? It's an eyebrow-raising twist
on an old favorite. And what a great
make-ahead dessert!*

1   cup sugar

1   can (12 ounces) evaporated
    milk

2   cups whole milk

4   egg yolks

⅓   cup butter, melted

4   tablespoons chocolate-
    flavored syrup

⅓   cup raisins

1   teaspoon vanilla extract

⅛   teaspoon ground cinnamon

⅛   teaspoon ground nutmeg

9   slices white bread, cubed

1   tablespoon semisweet
    chocolate chips

Preheat the oven to 400°F. In a large bowl, mix together the sugar, evaporated milk, whole milk, and egg yolks. Add the melted butter, chocolate syrup, raisins, vanilla extract, cinnamon, and nutmeg; mix. Add the bread cubes to the mixture and toss to saturate the bread. Pour the mixture into a greased 8-inch square baking pan. Sprinkle chips on top. Bake for 35 to 40 minutes or until lightly browned and set. Allow to cool before cutting. Cut into squares.

NOTE: This gets firmer and is easier to cut when cool. If you'd like to reheat it slightly before serving, just pop it in the microwave. If you'd like, serve it the old-fashioned way: topped with cream or milk.

chocolate peanut butter stripes

4 to 5 servings

*How about putting together two all-time favorites, chocolate
and peanut butter, in one delicious dessert?
It's a guaranteed winner!*

2 cups plus 2 tablespoons cold
milk, divided

2 tablespoons chunky peanut
butter

1 cup frozen whipped topping,
thawed (1 8-ounce container
equals 3½ cups)

1 package (4-serving size)
chocolate instant pudding
and pie filling

In a small bowl, combine 2 tablespoons milk with the peanut
butter; stir until well blended. Stir in the whipped topping. Using
the remaining 2 cups milk and the pudding mix, make the pudding
according to the package directions. Before allowing the mixture to
harden, spoon half of the pudding mixture into dessert glasses,
cover with the whipped topping mixture divided evenly among the
glasses, and top with the remaining pudding mixture. Keep chilled
until ready to serve.

quick-as-a-wink rice pudding
6 to 8 servings

*Think it takes hours to make rice pudding? This one's
sure to make you think again!*

1 package (4-serving size)
  instant vanilla pudding and
  pie filling

4 cups cold cooked rice
½ cup raisins

Make the pudding according to the package directions. Place the pudding in a medium-sized bowl and mix in the rice and raisins. Place in 6 to 8 individual serving glasses and serve immediately.

NOTE: You can use any rice, but I like to use the enriched whole-grain white rice. If you prepare this in advance, store it in the refrigerator and mix in additional prepared instant pudding just before serving.

puddings, sauces, and other yummies

holiday chocolate mousse

4 servings
(about 2 cups)

Bet you never thought of making mousse with caramel candies.
Well, you won't forget this one—
it's so rich and creamy!

1 package (7 to 9 ounces) chocolate-covered caramel candies

¼ cup heavy cream

1 tablespoon rum or ¼ teaspoon rum extract (optional)

1 container (8 ounces) frozen whipped topping, thawed

In a double boiler or nonstick saucepan, heat the caramels and heavy cream over low heat, stirring until smooth. Stir in the rum, then pour the mixture into a large bowl. Cool for 4 to 5 minutes, then fold in the whipped topping. Spoon into small dessert cups and chill for at least 1 hour before serving.

puddings, sauces, and other yummies

fruit cream
2 cups

Could there be an easier dip for fresh fruit?!

1 package (4-serving size)
instant vanilla pudding and
pie filling

1 pint sour cream

In a medium-sized bowl, mix together both ingredients. Serve immediately with fresh fruit or refrigerate until ready to serve.

sour cream dip

about 1 cup

It's always a good idea to have a container of sour cream on hand, 'cause you never know when company might stop by. And you'll always be ready for them, 'cause you can whip up this quick dip in no time!

¼ cup firmly packed brown sugar

½ teaspoon vanilla extract

1 cup (½ pint) sour cream

Combine all ingredients in a medium-sized bowl; stir to blend well. Chill until ready to serve.

NOTE: Serve as a dip with your favorite fresh fruits.

vanilla sauce

3 cups

*Here's an easy and delicious way to take plain cake or
fruit and make a yummy dessert—in a hurry!*

3½ cups cold milk

1 package (4-serving size)
   instant vanilla pudding
   and pie filling

1 teaspoon vanilla extract

2 to 3 tablespoons any flavor
  liqueur, such as coffee- or
  almond-flavored (optional)

Pour the milk into a large bowl. Add the pudding mix, vanilla extract, and liqueur and beat with a wire whisk until well blended. Let stand for 10 minutes until slightly thickened.

puddings, sauces, and other yummies

chocolate sauce

about 1½ cups

Don't get caught again without dessert. Whip this up in minutes and serve it over cake, bananas, strawberries, fresh fruit, ice cream . . . anything!

¾ cup sugar

1½ tablespoons unsalted butter

2 squares (1 ounce each) unsweetened baking chocolate, broken up

½ cup heavy cream

½ teaspoon vanilla extract

In a medium-sized saucepan, combine the sugar, butter, chocolate, and heavy cream. Cook over moderate heat, stirring constantly, until the mixture blends and comes to a boil. Let boil gently, without stirring, for 2 minutes. Remove from heat and stir in the vanilla extract. Serve warm.

puddings, sauces, and other yummies

berry sauces

Capture summer berries at their best!

blueberry lemon sauce
about 1½ cups

⅔ cup water

2 teaspoons sugar

2 teaspoons cornstarch

¼ teaspoon ground nutmeg

¼ teaspoon ground cinnamon

1 pint fresh blueberries, cleaned

¼ teaspoon grated lemon rind

¼ teaspoon lemon juice

In a large saucepan, combine the water, sugar, cornstarch, nutmeg, and cinnamon. Cook over medium heat, adding the blueberries and stirring until thickened. Stir in the lemon rind and juice. Pour into a small bowl, cover, and chill until ready to serve.

fresh strawberry sauce
about 2 cups

3 cups fresh strawberries, washed, hulled, and halved

2 tablespoons orange juice

1 tablespoon sugar

1 teaspoon grated orange rind

Blend all the ingredients in a blender or food processor. Pour into a small bowl, cover, and chill thoroughly before serving.

puddings, sauces, and other yummies

raspberry sauce
about 1½ cups

1 package (10 ounces) frozen   ¼ teaspoon almond extract
   raspberries in syrup, thawed

Blend the raspberries and almond extract until smooth, in a blender or food processor. If desired, press through a fine strainer to remove the seeds. Pour into a small bowl, cover, and chill until ready to serve.

NOTE: These are great fresh summertime toppings for desserts like pound cake or fresh fruit. For a quick "Peach Melba," slice one golden pound cake into individual servings, top each slice with a scoop of vanilla ice cream and fresh or canned sliced peaches, then drizzle with Raspberry Sauce. Mmmm!!

berry delight
about 2 cups

3 cups sliced strawberries   3 tablespoons water
6 tablespoons raspberry   ½ teaspoon ground cinnamon
   spreadable fruit

Combine all the ingredients in a medium-sized bowl, cover, and chill for one hour.

NOTE: Use to top slices of chocolate or golden pound cake. Then top each serving with a dollop of whipped topping!

easy peach topping

1 to 2 servings

You can't beat this for the quickest topping for French toast, waffles, or ice cream. And how 'bout stacking the peaches on plain cake and adding whipped topping for a fresh peach "shortcake"?

1 cup unpeeled peach slices   ⅛ teaspoon ground cinnamon

1 teaspoon lemon or lime juice   2 teaspoons sugar

Place the peach slices in a medium-sized bowl; sprinkle with the lemon juice, then with the cinnamon and sugar. Mix and set aside for 10 to 15 minutes to "marry" the flavors.

fluffy pudding frosting

4 cups

(enough for about 2 9" × 13" cakes)

*Here's one of those basic recipes that goes with so
many things—it's a must in every recipe box.
I know it'll be a "goody" for you.*

1 cup cold milk

1 package (4-serving size) any
flavor instant pudding and
pie filling

1 container (8 ounces) frozen
whipped topping, thawed

Pour the milk into a large bowl. Add the pudding mix and beat
with a wire whisk until well blended. Gently stir in the whipped
topping.

NOTE: Spread on cakes or cupcakes. Store the frosted cakes in the
refrigerator.

cream cheese frosting

about 3 cups
(enough for a 9" × 13" sheet cake)

*This goes great with No-Shortening Pineapple Cake
(see page 35) or almost any cake, especially
carrot, spice, and pumpkin. It'll
taste like you fussed, but
you'll know better!*

1   package (8 ounces) cream
cheese, softened

½   cup (1 stick) butter,
softened

1   box (16 ounces)
confectioners' sugar

1   tablespoon vanilla extract

½   to 1 cup chopped walnuts
(optional)

In a large bowl, beat the cream cheese and butter until smooth and creamy. Gradually beat in the sugar until well blended. Beat in the vanilla extract. Stir in the chopped walnuts, if desired.

puddings, sauces, and other yummies

strawberry trifle

6 to 8 servings

*An elegant dessert . . . in just minutes. And if you don't have
strawberries on hand? Any fresh or canned fruits
or fruit preserves will work.*

1 fresh or frozen pound cake, thawed

1 package (4-serving size) instant vanilla pudding and pie filling

2 cups strawberries, sliced and sugared to taste (about one tablespoon)

2 cups frozen whipped topping, thawed (an 8-ounce container equals 3½ cups)

¼ cup toasted slivered almonds (optional)

Fresh strawberries for garnish (optional)

Cut pound cake into 8 or 10 slices. Arrange half the slices in a 2-quart glass serving bowl, cutting the pieces to fit the bowl. Prepare the pudding according to the package directions. Spoon half the strawberries over the cake; spread with 1 cup pudding. Repeat with the remaining cake slices, strawberries, and pudding. Cover; chill for at least 4 hours. Spread the whipped topping over the trifle, sprinkle with slivered almonds, and garnish with fresh strawberries.

fast cobbler

4 to 6 servings

Remember all the wonderful things Grandma used to do with strawberries? Well, you can bring back those sweet memories without all the work.

½ cup (1 stick) butter, melted
1 cup self-rising flour
¾ cup sugar, divided
¾ cup milk

2 cups fresh strawberries, hulled, cleaned, and cut into quarters
½ cup water

Preheat the oven to 350°F. Pour the melted butter into a 1½-quart glass baking dish. In a large bowl, combine the flour, ¼ cup sugar, and milk, then pour evenly over the butter. In a separate bowl, combine the strawberries, remaining ½ cup sugar, and water; spoon evenly over the flour-milk layer. DO NOT STIR. Bake for 40 to 45 minutes or until golden. Serve warm or cold.

puddings, sauces, and other yummies

blueberry cobbler

4 servings

*It's a good thing they won't have to wait long for
this one—it's best eaten while still warm.*

COBBLER TOPPING

¾ cup all-purpose flour

3 tablespoons sugar

1½ teaspoons baking powder

¼ teaspoon ground cinnamon

¼ teaspoon salt

1 egg, beaten

⅓ cup milk

⅓ to ½ cup sugar

1 tablespoon cornstarch

3 cups fresh or frozen and thawed blueberries

4 teaspoons lemon juice

1 teaspoon grated lemon peel

⅛ teaspoon salt

In a medium-sized bowl, make the Cobbler Topping by stirring together the flour, 3 tablespoons sugar, baking powder, cinnamon, and ¼ teaspoon salt. Combine the egg and milk; stir into the flour mixture just until moistened. Set aside. Preheat the oven to 375°F. In a saucepan, combine the sugar and cornstarch; add the blueberries, lemon juice, lemon peel, and salt. Cook over medium heat, stirring, for 4 to 6 minutes or until thickened. Pour the mixture into a 2-quart baking dish; spoon the Cobbler Topping over. Bake for 15 to 20 minutes or until golden brown.

NOTE: If you make this in advance, just reheat it and serve warm with ice cream or whipped cream.

puddings, sauces, and other yummies

summer fruit stack

about 8 servings

This is always a popular recipe because it's easy to make it your own. Use whatever fruit you've got on hand—from berries to melon and anything in between.

1 angel food cake (10 to 12 ounces)

1 package (8 ounces) cream cheese, softened

½ cup milk

1 cup confectioners' sugar

1 container (8 ounces) frozen whipped topping, thawed

5 to 6 unpeeled peaches, plums, or nectarines (or a combination), sliced or chunked

Tear the angel food cake into little pieces and place in a large bowl. Add the remaining ingredients, except the fruit, and mix. In a large glass serving bowl, alternate layers of cake mixture and fruit.

NOTE: A store-bought angel food cake is just right for this.

pinwheel cake and cream

about 12 servings

*It's easy to be creative with this one. It can be
whatever you want, so go for it!*

2 cups cold skim milk

1 package (4-serving size)
   instant vanilla pudding and
   pie filling

1 cup light frozen whipped
   topping, thawed (an 8-ounce
   container equals 3½ cups)

1 teaspoon grated orange peel

1 nectarine, peach, or plum,
   cut into bite-sized slices

1 light or regular golden pound
   cake (about 12 ounces),
   sliced

2 cups cut summer fruit*

Pour the milk into a large bowl. Add the pudding mix and beat
to blend well, about 3 minutes. Allow to sit for 5 minutes to thicken
slightly. Stir in the whipped topping, grated orange peel, and fruit
slices. Arrange the pound cake slices in a pinwheel design by over-
lapping them on a large serving plate. Spoon pudding mixture
evenly over cake slices. Top with the 2 cups cut summer fruit and
serve.

NOTE: If making this ahead, chill after spooning the pudding mixture over the cake, then top with the 2 cups fruit just before serving.

*I like to use a sliced peach, and ½ cup each of strawberries, seedless grapes, and
raspberries. You can also use nectarines, plums, and blueberries.

puddings, sauces, and other yummies

easy peach fancy

6 to 9 servings

This freezes well, so it's a great make-ahead—but you might want to make extra because they'll gobble it up before you can get it into the freezer!

1 cup sugar	2 to 3 peaches, halved and pitted
½ cup (1 stick) butter	
1 cup all-purpose flour	1 teaspoon lemon juice
1 teaspoon baking powder	½ teaspoon sugar
2 eggs	¼ teaspoon ground cinnamon

Preheat the oven to 350°F. In a large bowl, cream together the sugar and butter. Add the flour, baking powder, and eggs; beat well. (The batter will be thick.) Spread the batter into an 8-inch square baking pan that has been coated with nonstick vegetable spray. Cover with the peach halves, skin side up, so that they are just touching (do not crowd). Sprinkle the peaches with the lemon juice, then sprinkle with the sugar and cinnamon. Bake for about 1 hour or until golden. Remove from the oven and cool on a rack. Serve warm or cold.

NOTE: You can use nectarines or plums instead of peaches, or even try a combination. You may want to serve this at room temperature or reheated.

puddings, sauces, and other yummies

apple kuchen
about 6 servings

*Remember the kuchen Grandma used to make? This'll
sure bring back happy memories.*

½ cup (1 stick) butter, melted

½ cup sugar, plus 4
tablespoons, divided

1 cup all-purpose flour

1 teaspoon baking powder

1 teaspoon vanilla extract

1 egg, beaten

8 large Granny Smith apples,
peeled, cored, and cut into
thick slices

¼ teaspoon ground cinnamon

3 tablespoons slivered
almonds

Preheat the oven to 350°F. In a large bowl, mix together the
butter, ½ cup sugar, flour, baking powder, vanilla extract, and egg.
Pour half the batter into a greased 8-inch square baking pan and
spread to cover bottom. In another large bowl, toss the apple slices
with the remaining 4 tablespoons sugar and the cinnamon, then
place on top of the batter in the baking pan. Spread the remaining
batter over the apple mixture. Bake for 20 minutes, then sprinkle
with almonds and bake for 30 minutes more.

puddings, sauces, and other yummies

grape brûlée

about 4 servings

*With just a few ingredients, you can have the
quickest, most elegant dessert.*

2 cups seedless red or green
grapes

1 container (16 ounces) sour
cream

¼ cup granulated brown sugar

Preheat the oven to broil. Wash and stem the grapes, then place them in an 8-inch square broiler-proof baking pan. Cover with the sour cream and top with the brown sugar. Place the baking dish under the broiler for about 10 minutes or until the sour cream and sugar become bubbly. Chill thoroughly before serving.

puddings, sauces, and other yummies

mint cookie dessert

9 to 12 servings

*This one is sure to please kids of all ages, 'cause it combines
everybody's favorites. It's a great make-ahead,
too—let it sit overnight in the fridge
and boy, oh boy, what a treat!*

32 chocolate sandwich cookies
   (1 16-ounce package
   contains about 42 cookies)
1   pint heavy cream

2 cups miniature
  marshmallows
1 cup pastel pillow-shaped
  after-dinner mints

In a food processor or blender, finely crush the cookies. Place
half the crushed cookies in a 9" × 13" baking pan. In a medium-
sized bowl, whip the heavy cream; fold in the marshmallows and
mints. Spread the whipped cream mixture over the crushed cookie
layer. Sprinkle the remaining crushed cookies on top. Refrigerate
overnight before serving.

puddings, sauces, and other yummies

chocolate peanut butter clusters

about 60

The kids will think these are magic—and they are.
Why, you'll make them in a flash and then
they'll disappear just as fast!!

1¼ cups (1 6-ounce package)
 semisweet chocolate chips

1 package (12 ounces)
 peanut butter chips

½ cup peanut butter

1 package (11 ounces) salted
 peanuts (2⅓ cups)

 In a large glass bowl, combine the chocolate and peanut butter chips. Cover; microwave for 2 to 3 minutes or until partially melted. Stir, then add the peanut butter. Microwave 2 to 3 minutes more. Remove from microwave, then stir in the peanuts with a wooden spoon. Drop by teaspoonfuls onto waxed paper and refrigerate until set.

puddings, sauces, and other yummies

cookie clusters

4 to 5 dozen

*These are fun as is, but you can make them extra fun
and colorful by sprinkling on a little shredded
coconut, colored sprinkles, or chopped Heath® candy bars
before they cool.*

12 ounces white chocolate melting wafers, chips, or squares

2 tablespoons peanut butter

1¼ cups Rice Krispies® cereal

1 cup Spanish (red-skinned) peanuts

1 cup miniature marshmallows

Melt the chocolate with the peanut butter in a microwave (or in a saucepan over low heat, stirring frequently); do not allow the mixture to boil. Let cool slightly, then stir in the cereal and peanuts. Fold in the marshmallows, then drop the mixture by teaspoonfuls onto waxed paper. Allow to cool at room temperature for at least 20 to 30 minutes before serving.

NOTE: These will keep for up to two weeks in the refrigerator.

family favorites

death by chocolate

serves up to 24
(or 1 serious chocoholic!)

*Here's one of my most requested recipes of all time. Sinfully
delicious, easy, and convenient ('cause you can make
it in advance), it's the ultimate—the one
everybody goes crazy for. Be ready
for lots of applause.*

1 box (19.8 ounces) fudge brownie mix

¼ to ½ cup coffee liqueur

3 packages (4-serving size each) instant chocolate mousse

8 chocolate-covered toffee candy bars (1.4 ounces each) (like SKOR® or Heath® Bars)

1 large container (12 ounces) frozen whipped topping, thawed

Bake the brownies according to the brownie package directions; let cool. Prick holes in the tops of the brownies with a fork and pour the coffee liqueur over the brownies; set aside. Prepare the chocolate mousse according to the package directions. Break the candy bars into small pieces in a food processor or by gently tapping the wrapped bars with a hammer. Break up half the brownies into small pieces and place in the bottom of a large glass bowl or trifle dish. Cover with half the mousse, then half the candy, and then half the whipped topping. Repeat layers with the remaining ingredients.

NOTE: Instead of the coffee liqueur, you may substitute a mixture of 1 teaspoon sugar and 4 tablespoons leftover black coffee, or just leave out the coffee flavoring entirely.

chocolate chip cheesecake

15 to 20 servings

*A classic! A favorite! And incredibly delicious! This simple
Chocolate Chip Cheesecake is sure
to become your standard.*

3 packages (8 ounces each)
   cream cheese, softened

3 eggs

¾ cup sugar

1 teaspoon vanilla extract

2 rolls (20 ounces each)
   refrigerator chocolate chip
   cookie dough

Preheat the oven to 350°F. In a large bowl, beat together the cream cheese, eggs, sugar, and vanilla extract until well mixed; set aside. Slice the cookie dough rolls into ⅓-inch slices. Arrange the slices from one roll on the bottom of a greased 9" × 13" glass baking dish; press together so there are no holes in the dough. Spoon the cream cheese mixture evenly over the dough; top with the remaining slices of cookie dough. Bake for 45 to 50 minutes, or until golden and the center is slightly firm. Remove from the oven, let cool, then refrigerate. Cut into slices when well chilled.

NOTE: Keep the cookie dough refrigerated until just before slicing. You can serve the cheesecake plain, with chocolate sauce, with fudge or whipped topping—whatever's your favorite.

chocolate sour cream cake

6 to 9 servings

*This is a chocolate version of the traditional sour cream
cake, and it's sure to start a new tradition.*

1 cup all-purpose flour	1 teaspoon baking soda
1 cup sugar	3 tablespoons baking cocoa
1 cup sour cream	¼ teaspoon salt
1 egg	

Preheat the oven to 350°F. In a large bowl, mix together all the
ingredients. Beat until smooth and thoroughly combined. Pour the
mixture into a greased 8-inch square baking pan and bake for
about 30 minutes or until a wooden toothpick inserted in the center
comes out clean.

NOTE: Top with whipped topping or Cream Cheese Frosting (see
page 110). If you'd like, top with a sprinkle of confectioners' sugar
or some ground cinnamon and granulated sugar.

brownie cheesecake bars

24 to 36 bars

*Is there anybody who doesn't like brownies? Nah! Is there
anybody who doesn't like cheesecake? Nah! Put 'em
together and . . . Wow! Wow! Wow!!*

1 box (19.8 ounces) fudge
  brownie mix

1 package (8 ounces) cream
  cheese, softened

2 tablespoons margarine

1 tablespoon cornstarch

1 can (14 ounces) sweetened
  condensed milk

1 egg

1 teaspoon vanilla extract

Preheat the oven to 350°F. Prepare the brownie mix according
to the package directions and spread the batter in a greased 9" ×
13" baking pan. In a small bowl, beat the cream cheese, margarine,
and cornstarch until fluffy. Gradually beat in the sweetened condensed milk, then the egg and vanilla extract. Pour evenly over the
brownie batter and bake for 50 to 60 minutes or until the top is
lightly browned. Let cool, then chill. Cut into bars and store, covered, in the refrigerator.

eclair cake

15 to 20 servings

*Scrumptious! Without a doubt, this one's a winner 'cause
it's like creamy eclairs plus, plus, plus . . .*

1 cup water	3 packages (4-serving size each) instant vanilla pudding and pie filling
½ cup (1 stick) butter	
1 cup all-purpose flour	1 container (8 ounces) frozen whipped topping, thawed
4 eggs	
12 ounces cream cheese, softened	Chocolate-flavored syrup for topping
4½ cups milk	Slivered almonds for garnish (optional)

Preheat the oven to 400°F. Place the water in a medium-sized saucepan; heat until moderately hot. Reduce heat to low, add the butter and melt. Remove the saucepan from the stovetop, then add the flour and beat lightly. Add the eggs, one at a time, beating well. Spread the mixture on the bottom of a lightly greased 10" × 15" baking pan. Bake for 20 to 25 minutes, or until golden and brown on the edges; let cool, then transfer to a serving platter. Meanwhile, place the cream cheese in a large bowl and beat, then add the milk and vanilla pudding mix. Beat for about 2 minutes or until thick, then spread over the baked mixture. Refrigerate for at least 1 hour to set. Spread the top with the whipped topping, then drizzle with the chocolate syrup. Garnish with slivered almonds, if desired.

peanut butter chocolate candy cookies

25 to 30 bars

*Wait'll you taste these! They're one of my most popular
recipes of all time, so they're sure to become
a favorite at your house, too.*

1 cup creamy peanut butter

½ pound (2 sticks) butter, melted

1 pound confectioners' sugar (about 2½ cups)

1 cup graham cracker crumbs

1 package (12 ounces) chocolate chips, melted

In a large bowl, mix together the peanut butter, butter, confectioners' sugar, and graham cracker crumbs. Spread the mixture in a well-greased 10" × 15" baking pan. Pour the melted chocolate chips evenly over the mixture. Refrigerate for 15 minutes. Slice into bars, but leave in the pan. Refrigerate until well chilled; serve cold.

NOTE: To melt chocolate chips, place them in a glass bowl, cover it, and microwave until melted, stirring occasionally.

ice cream brownie bowl

10 to 12 servings

*Here's a way to make a couple of everyday desserts into one
very special dessert—great for a special day
(or for making any day special!).*

1   package (21½ ounces)
    brownie mix

⅓ cup Heath® bits

About 1 quart vanilla ice
    cream, softened

About 2 cups whipped cream or
    whipped topping

Prepare the brownies according to the package directions, folding the Heath® bits into the batter, and bake in a greased 9" × 13" baking pan. Underbake the brownies slightly (for a chewier consistency) and cool thoroughly. Meanwhile, line a round bowl (about 2½ quarts) with plastic wrap. Place about ⅔ of the brownies into the bowl in big chunks; press the brownies together, molding them to the bowl, up to about an inch from the top of the bowl. Spoon the vanilla ice cream into the bowl, and press it firmly over the brownie crust, completely covering it. Place the remaining brownies over the top and press firmly into the ice cream. Cover with plastic wrap and freeze overnight. To serve: Remove the top layer of plastic wrap, invert the bowl onto a serving platter, and thaw for about 10 minutes. Then wrap the bowl with a warm dish towel and let stand for a few minutes more. Remove the bowl, then the remaining plastic wrap. Cover the top with whipped cream.

NOTE: How 'bout topping it with chocolate sprinkles or more Heath® bits?

crustless cheesecake

6 to 8 servings

*Still an all-time favorite with everybody—it was my very first
overwhelming hit recipe. And the reasons: great taste,
great looks, and easy-as-can-be!*

2 packages (8 ounces each)
cream cheese, softened

⅔ cup sugar

3 eggs

½ teaspoon vanilla extract

¼ teaspoon fresh lemon juice

TOPPING

2 cups (16 ounces) sour
cream

3 tablespoons sugar

1 teaspoon vanilla extract

¼ teaspoon fresh lemon juice

Preheat the oven to 325°F. Put the cream cheese and sugar in
a large bowl and beat well. Beat in the eggs, one at a time. Beat
in the vanilla extract and lemon juice. Spoon the mixture into a
greased 9-inch glass pie plate. Bake for 45 to 50 minutes, until
golden brown. Remove from the oven and let cool for 10 to 15
minutes. (Do not turn off oven.) Meanwhile, in another large bowl,
mix together the Topping ingredients. Spread over the top of the
cheesecake and bake for 10 minutes longer. (The top will remain
almost liquid.) Let cool, then refrigerate for 4 hours or overnight.

NOTE: I like to cover the cheesecake with canned filling or fresh
berries before serving it.

my peanut butter pie

6 to 8 servings

*A peanut-y treat that always gets raves, whether it's for
a snack or dessert . . . well, look how many
of us love peanut butter!!*

1 cup confectioners' sugar

½ cup peanut butter

1 9-inch pie crust, baked and
cooled, according to
package directions

1 package (4-serving size)
vanilla instant pudding and
pie filling

4 ounces frozen whipped
topping, thawed (½ of an
8-ounce container)

In a medium-sized bowl, combine the confectioners' sugar and
peanut butter. Mix to a crumbly consistency (like a streusel) and
remove about ½ cup of the mixture; cover and set aside for later
use. Pour the remaining mixture evenly over the pie crust. Make
the pudding according to the package directions; pour the pudding
over the crumb layer, then cover and refrigerate overnight. Before
serving, cover with whipped topping and top with the reserved peanut butter mixture.

strawberry "pizza"

about 12 servings

*What an elegant, fun dessert! And it's colorful enough
to be the dessert table centerpiece.*

1¼ cups confectioners' sugar, divided	1 teaspoon vanilla extract
1 cup all-purpose flour	1 container (8 ounces) frozen whipped topping, thawed
½ cup margarine or butter, softened	1 pint fresh strawberries, hulled, cleaned, and sliced
1 package (8 ounces) cream cheese, softened	

Preheat the oven to 350°F. In a medium-sized bowl, make a soft dough by mixing together ¼ cup confectioners' sugar, flour, and margarine. Spread the dough onto a 12-inch greased pizza pan and bake for 20 to 25 minutes or until golden. Let cool. Meanwhile, in a large bowl, combine the cream cheese, remaining 1 cup confectioners' sugar, and vanilla extract. Mix well, then fold in the whipped topping. Spread the mixture over the cooled crust, then top with sliced strawberries. Refrigerate for 2 hours before serving.

NOTE: You can use almost any single fruit or combination. This will keep for several days in the refrigerator.

banana trifle

12 to 16 servings

*Wanna be ready for spur-of-the-moment entertaining?
By keeping these few, simple ingredients on hand,
you can be. (People will think you've
been waiting for them!)*

1 package (11 to 12 ounces) vanilla wafers, coarsely crushed, divided

3 packages (4-serving size each) instant vanilla pudding and pie filling

5 cups milk

1 large container (12 ounces) frozen whipped topping, thawed

1 cup (½ pint) sour cream

2 to 3 bananas, sliced

Dash of ground nutmeg (optional)

Reserve ½ cup coarsely crushed vanilla wafers; place the remaining crushed wafers in a 9" × 13" baking pan. In a large bowl, combine the pudding mix and milk; beat until smooth and thickened, 1 to 2 minutes. Add half the whipped topping (about 2¼ cups) and the sour cream; mix well. Place half the pudding mixture (about 4 cups) over the crushed wafers and smooth. Arrange banana slices over the pudding mixture. Smooth over that the remaining pudding mixture. Cover the pudding with the remaining whipped topping. Finely crush the reserved ½ cup wafers and sprinkle over the whipped topping; garnish with a dash of nutmeg, if desired.

NOTE: One 11- to 12-ounce package of vanilla wafers yields about 5 cups of coarsely crushed wafers.

grated apple pie

6 to 8 servings

You have to try this one—it actually won an apple pie
contest. Of course, you'll need to try serving
it your own favorite ways . . . with
Cheddar cheese, or ice cream,
or whipped cream, or . . .

1¼ cups sugar	½ cup (1 stick) butter or margarine, melted
3 tablespoons all-purpose flour	1 teaspoon vanilla extract
½ teaspoon ground cinnamon	3 cups coarsely grated apples
½ teaspoon ground nutmeg	1 9-inch deep dish pie crust
2 eggs, beaten	

Preheat the oven to 400°F. In a large bowl, combine the sugar, flour, cinnamon, and nutmeg. Add the eggs, butter, and vanilla extract, then fold in the apples. Pour the mixture into the pie crust and bake for 10 minutes. Reduce the heat to 350°F. and bake for 60 to 65 minutes more or until golden on top. Cool completely and serve.

key lime pie
6 to 8 servings

*Not only is this the preferred dessert in the Florida Keys, it's a
favorite at my house, too. And no cooking . . . Yippee!!
Have fun! (Don't add green food color—true
Key Lime Pie is not green.)*

1 can (14 ounces) sweetened
condensed milk

1 tablespoon grated lime rind

2 egg yolks, slightly beaten

½ cup lime juice

1 prepared 9-inch graham
cracker pie crust

In a large bowl, mix together the sweetened condensed milk,
lime rind, and egg yolks. Stir in the lime juice and continue stirring
until the mixture has thickened. Pour into the pie crust and chill
for 3 hours before serving.

NOTE: You can serve this plain or with whipped cream, or you can
garnish it with some extra grated lime rind. And in case you were
wondering, no baking is needed because thickening is a result of
the reaction of the milk with the lime juice. As with any dish con-
taining raw eggs, be sure to store this in the refrigerator until ready
to serve.

pudding pecan pie

6 to 8 servings

*When we think about "favorite desserts" we've got to include
Pecan Pie. Too hard? Too heavy? Here's a way to
have it easier and lighter, while still holding
on to that "yesterday" taste.*

1 package (4-serving size) instant or regular vanilla or butterscotch pudding and pie filling

1 cup light corn syrup

¾ cup evaporated milk

1 egg, slightly beaten

1 cup chopped pecans or walnuts

1 unbaked 9-inch pie shell

Preheat the oven to 375°F. In a medium-sized bowl, blend the pudding mix with the corn syrup, using an electric mixer on low speed. Gradually add the evaporated milk and egg, beating until well blended. Stir in the pecans. Pour the mixture into the pie shell and bake for about 40 minutes or until the top is firm and just begins to crack. Remove from the oven and cool for at least 3 to 4 hours before serving.

refreshing changes

blender fruit drink
about 6 cups

*What a perfect way to enjoy the freshness of
summer any time of the year.*

1 can (29 ounces) fruit
cocktail

½ cup sour cream

4 tablespoons grenadine or
cherry juice (from a
maraschino cherry jar)

2 cups fresh, diced fruit

Place all the ingredients in a blender jar and blend until smooth. Serve chilled.

NOTE: You may want to add a few tablespoons of sugar and maybe the juice of half a lemon or lime along with the sugar. Experiment until you find your favorite way!

frosty apple drink

4½ cups

Frosty, smooth and fresh . . . so how 'bout an apple lift?

1 pint plus 4 to 6 scoops vanilla ice cream or frozen yogurt

1 pint chilled apple cider

½ teaspoon ground nutmeg, plus extra for garnish, if desired

Allow the pint of ice cream to stand at room temperature until fairly soft. Place in a blender jar and blend. Add the cider gradually and continue blending until thoroughly mixed and frothy. Stir in the nutmeg. Pour into tall glasses or mugs and top each serving with a scoop of ice cream and a sprinkle of nutmeg, if you'd like. Serve immediately.

sunshine banana smoothie
about 3 cups

Here's a frothy snack that's full of flavor and everything that's good for you.

1 peeled frozen banana, broken into chunks

4 to 5 fresh strawberries

1 cup orange juice

1 teaspoon creamy peanut butter (optional)

Combine all the ingredients in a blender, and blend until smooth.

NOTE: The frozen banana keeps the smoothie from being watered down, because it takes the place of ice. To freeze bananas: Place peeled bananas on a cookie sheet, cover, and freeze for about 2 hours. To store, place the bananas in a plastic bag and keep frozen until ready to use. Peeled, frozen bananas keep for two weeks in the freezer. You can also substitute your favorite fruits (that you've frozen like the bananas) or juices.

apple honey cooler

about 6 servings
(6 cups)

So different! So easy! So refreshing!

1 quart chilled apple cider or juice

2 cups chilled fresh-squeezed orange juice

¼ cup honey

2 teaspoons grated orange rind

Apple slices for garnish

Combine all the ingredients in a large covered container or bowl and shake or stir to blend. Pour over ice in tall glasses. Garnish each glass with an apple slice.

peach frosty

2 servings

*It's like drinking fresh peaches, so
enjoy the best of summer!*

1 cup sliced peaches	1 teaspoon vanilla extract
6 tablespoons confectioners' sugar	¼ to ½ teaspoon ground ginger
½ cup milk	1 cup vanilla ice cream

Place the peach slices, confectioners' sugar, and milk in a blender; purée until smooth. Add the remaining ingredients and blend until smooth. Pour into tall glasses and serve immediately.

NOTE: If you want, you can cut down on calories by using skim milk instead of whole milk, and ice milk instead of ice cream. You can make these look extra festive if you garnish with additional peach slices, some berries, or whipped cream.

florida "champagne"

40 half-cup servings

*A smart party drink that calls for
its own celebration . . .*

1 cup sugar

3 cups water

2 liters ginger ale, chilled, plus
extra for ice mold

Orange slices (optional)

Maraschino cherries (optional)

4 cups cranberry juice, chilled

4 cups pineapple juice, chilled

2 cups orange juice, chilled

In a medium-sized saucepan, combine the sugar and water; boil for 3 minutes or until syrupy. Chill. Meanwhile, combine the extra ginger ale with the orange slices and cherries in a mold; freeze. Combine the chilled sugar-water mixture and juices in a large punch bowl. Before serving, add the 2 liters of chilled ginger ale and the ice mold. (As the ice mold melts, the punch keeps its flavor and isn't diluted as it would be with regular ice.)

party mulled cider

12 to 16 servings

Perfect for winter, or anytime you want a warm,
cozy treat for all of your senses.

1 gallon fresh apple cider	¼ teaspoon ground nutmeg
3 2-inch cinnamon sticks	½ to 1 cup light brown sugar (to taste)
⅛ teaspoon allspice	
16 whole cloves	

Pour the cider into a large pot. Place the remaining ingredients in a cheesecloth bag and tie closed. Place in the pot and simmer for about 1 hour. Remove the cheesecloth bag. Pour into mugs and serve.

Index

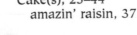

Fruit (*cont.*)
  trifle, 111
  vanilla sauce for, 104
  see also specific fruits
Fudge:
  cake, low-fat chocolate, 29
  pudding cake, easy, 27

Graham cracker treats, 79
Grape brûlée, 118
Grated apple pie, 136

Halloween bars, 83
Heat distribution, in ovens, 19
Holiday cake, 44
Holiday chocolate mousse, 101
Honey apple cooler, 144

Ice cream:
  brownie bowl, 131
  chocolate sauce for, 105
  easy peach topping for, 108
  frosty apple drink, 142
  krispy cream pie, 64
  peach frosty, 145
Impossible chocolate cream pie,
    55
Information, 17–23
  baking, 19–21
  ingredient substitutions, 22
  packaged foods, 23
  weights and measures, 23
Ingredient substitutions, 22
Italian cheese pie, 62

Java chocolate cake, 28

Key lime pie, 137
Krispy cream pie, 64
Kuchen, apple, 117

Lemon:
  blueberry loaf, 88
  blueberry sauce, 106
  pudding cake, 30
  squares, 82
Lime pie, key, 137
Low-fat chocolate fudge cake, 29

Measures, 23
Melon chiffon cake, 34
Meringue cookies, 71
Mint cookie dessert, 119
Mix, meaning of, 21
Molasses cookies, soft, 72
"Mom's vacation" dessert, 65
Mousse:
  death by chocolate, 125
  holiday chocolate, 101
Muffins, 92–93
  easy banana, 92
  spicy carrot, 93
Mulled cider, party, 147
My peanut butter pie, 133

Nectarine(s):
  fancy, easy, 116
  pinwheel cake and cream, 115
  summer fruit stack, 114
No-bake cheesecake, 58
  double chocolate, 59
No-shortening pineapple cake,
    35
Nut(s):
  amazin' raisin cake, 37
  apple bars, 80
  apple scrounge, 81
  apple snack cake, 38
  brown sugar brownies, 78
  cherry bread, 90
  chocolate on chocolate pie, 54
  chocolate peanut butter clus-
    ters, 120
  cookie clusters, 121
  cream cheese frosting, 110
  no-shortening pineapple cake,
    35
  pudding pecan pie, 138
  raisin pumpkin cake, 40

Oatmeal bars, 84
One-dish strawberry pie, 50
Ovens, heat distribution in, 19

Packaged foods, sizes of, 23
Pans, cake, 19
Paradise fruit cake, 36

Raisin:
    cake, amazin', 37
    pumpkin cake, 40
Raspberry(ies):
    berry delight, 107
    sauce, 106–107
Rice pudding, quick-as-a-wink,
        100
Ricotta cheese:
    Christmas crunch cake, 42
    pie, Italian, 62

Sauces, 102–108
    berry, 106–107
    berry delight, 107
    blueberry lemon, 106
    chocolate, 105
    easy peach topping, 108
    fresh strawberry, 106
    fruit cream, 102
    raspberry, 106–107
    sour cream dip, 103
    vanilla, 104
Scotch spice cake, 43
Scrounge, apple, 81
"Shortcake," fresh peach, 108
Simple cheesecake pie, 57
Smoothie, sunshine banana, 143
Snack cake, apple, 38
Soft molasses cookies, 72
Soft peanut butter cookies, 75
Sour cream:
    chocolate cake, 127
    dip, 103
    pie, 63
Spice cake, scotch, 43
Spicy carrot muffins, 93
Sponge cookies, 77
Squares:
    graham cracker treats, 79
    lemon, 82
Stir, meaning of, 21
Storage, of baked goods, 20
Strawberry(ies):
    berry delight, 107

bread, 89
chocolate sauce for, 105
cream pie, 51
fast cobbler, 112
"Mom's vacation" dessert, 65
pie, one-dish, 50
"pizza," 134
sauce, fresh, 106
sponge cookies with topping
        and, 77
trifle, 111
Substitutions, ingredient, 22
Sugar cookies, 76
Summer fruit stack, 114
Sundae tarts, banana, 66
Sunshine banana smoothie, 143

Tart(s):
    banana sundae, 66
    blueberry, 67
    "Mom's vacation" dessert, 65
    use of word, 20
    see also Pies
Topping:
    easy peach, 108
    see also Sauces
Trifle:
    banana, 135
    strawberry, 111

Upside-down cake, apple, 39

Vanilla sauce, 104

Walnut(s):
    amazin' raisin cake, 37
    apple scrounge, 81
    cream cheese frosting, 110
    pudding pie, 138
Weights, 23
Whip, meaning of, 21

Yogurt:
    frosty apple drink, 142
    pumpkin pie, 53

ABOUT THE AUTHOR

Art Ginsburg is best known as TV's lovable cooking celebrity, MR. FOOD®. His popular food news insert segment is the largest in the nation, seen in over 260 cities.

Twelve years ago Art became MR. FOOD®, but long before that his life centered around food . . . and family. From running the family butcher shop to establishing the family catering business, Art has cultivated his many successes with his family by his side. Art's wife and three children all continue to work with him now in producing the MR. FOOD® television show, and his granddaughters appear to be Pop-Pop's three most enthusiastic fans.

Get All Five Books
in the Mr. Food® Library!

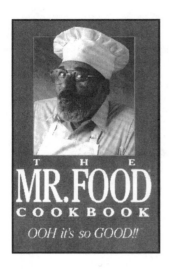

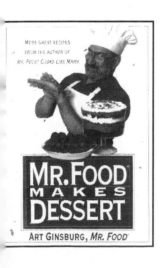

ENJOY THE *ENTIRE*
MR. FOOD®
EXPERIENCE!

y be satisfied with just a "taste" when you can have the entire "meal"? Once you've experienced any one
MR. FOOD®'s easy, tantalizing recipes, you'll want to try all of them! All you have to do is use this handy
m to order lots more **OOH it's so GOOD!!**™ (*And if you purchase 3 or more books with this order, you get
onus discount of $1.00 off the price of each book!*)

ase indicate the quantity of each **MR. FOOD®** Cookbook that you wish to order:

_____	The **MR. FOOD®** Cookbook, OOH it's so GOOD!!™ @ $12.95 each:	$ _____
_____	**MR. FOOD®** Cooks Like Mama @ $12.95 each:	_____
_____	**MR. FOOD®** Cooks Chicken @ $9.95 each:	_____
_____	**MR. FOOD®** Cooks Pasta @ $9.95 each:	_____
_____	**MR. FOOD®** Makes Dessert @ $9.95 each:	_____

+$2.00 <u>PER BOOK</u> Shipping & Handling
(*Canadian Orders add additional
$2.00 per book*)   _____

SUBTOTAL   _____

*Less $1.00 per book if
ordering 3 or more books*   _____

+ Applicable Sales Tax
(*FL Residents Only*)   _____

TOTAL - *In U.S. Funds* $ _____

ke check out to **MR. FOOD®** and send to: **MR. FOOD®**, P.O. Box 16216, Plantation, FL, 33318-6216

thod of Payment: _____   Check or Money Order Enclosed

_____ Credit Card: _____ Visa   _____ Mastercard

iration Date _____

nature _____

ount #

PLEASE ALLOW 6 TO 8 WEEKS FOR DELIVERY.